Stumpwork
& GOLDWORK EMBROIDERY

Dedication
To my dear travelling companion Katie
— with love.

Stumpwork

& GOLDWORK EMBROIDERY

inspired by Turkish, Syrian & Persian Tiles

Jane Nicholas

SALLYMILNER
PUBLISHING

First published in 2010 by

Sally Milner Publishing Pty Ltd

734 Woodville Road

Binda NSW 2583 AUSTRALIA

Reprinted 2010

© Jane Nicholas 2010

Design: Caroline Verity

Editing: Anne Savage

Photography: Tim Connolly

Illustration: Anna Warren, Warren Ventures, and Wendy Gorton

Printed in China

National Library of Australia Cataloguing-in-Publication entry

Author:	Nicholas, Jane.
Title:	Stumpwork & goldwork embroidery inspired by Turkish, Syrian & Persian tiles / Jane Nicholas.
ISBN:	9781863514095 (pbk.)
Series:	Milner craft series.
Notes:	Bibliography.
Subjects:	Stump work.
	Embroidery.
Dewey Number:	746.44

10 9 8 7 6 5 4 3 2

ACKNOWLEDGEMENTS

The response to the 'Tiles' has been heartening. I would like to
extend my gratitude to all those people who continue to share their passion
for stumpwork embroidery with me. Whether by correspondence or in class,
your enthusiasm provides invaluable motivation.

My wonderful family continues to provide wholehearted support and
encouragement for my work. Special thanks to John, who makes all the kits and
runs the mail order service with amazing efficiency and attention to detail.

Thank you to Avril Ambrose-De Haviland for enhancing
my knowledge of embroidered book covers.

Sincere thanks to my dear 'sewing friends' for their companionship
and the opportunity to share ideas and cherished stitching time.

Finally, to all those involved in the production of this
book at Sally Milner Publishing—your expertise, and belief
in my work, is sincerely appreciated.

Jane Nicholas

CONTENTS

Introduction

Originally intended to occupy a small chapter at the end of my book, Stumpwork Medieval Flora, published in 2009, my stumpwork embroidered tiles have taken on a life of their own, blossoming into a volume in their own right.

The research and embroidery involved in creating the designs for this book have been a joy—I have revelled in the opportunity to indulge a passion of mine since childhood—combining jewel-like colours, gold metallic threads and glittering beads. Sixteen projects are presented in this book, varying both in size and complexity. Each has been inspired by an example of Islamic art—pottery, textiles, manuscripts or jewellery—from Turkey, Syria, Persia, Arabia or India.

I am often asked about the source of my designs—where do the ideas come from? In this instance, it is the accumulation of a lifetime's fascination with 'things exotic'—from the Tales of the Arabian Nights (Sinbad, Aladdin, Ali Baba) as a child, to the discovery of the world of Diaghilev and his Ballets Russes at exhibitions held at the National Gallery of Australia—'From Studio to Stage in 1990', and 'From Russia with Love in 1998'—all gathered into the ever-expanding collection of books, catalogues, cuttings, postcards and photographs that make up my 'ideas journals'. I can still remember wandering into the Gallery of Islamic Art at the Victoria and Albert Museum, on a Churchill Fellowship in 1999, and being completely enchanted by the treasures on display there—from Islamic Spain and Morocco in the west to Afghanistan and Uzbekistan in the east. I am indeed fortunate to have also had the opportunity to travel to such magical places as India, Morocco and Turkey with my daughter, Katie. It has been a privilege to experience, first hand, many of the wonders of Islamic art.

It was while attending a course in 2001 that I went searching for an idea for an embroidered book cover—it was to be inspired by the jewelled and enamelled book covers of the Persian and Ottoman Empires and worked on velvet with gold metallic threads, silks and beads. I turned to my well-thumbed reference book, Pattern Design by Archibald H. Christie (first published in 1929), and found a drawing of a sixteenth century Turkish tile held by the Victoria and Albert Museum. I had my inspiration! I adapted this design for use as a book cover then created another two versions—one being for an embroidered panel inside the lid of a box and the other becoming the Turkish Tulip Tile featured in the first section of the book. I have included images of all three versions of this design, plus the drawing of the original tile, to illustrate how objects from the past can still inform our work today.

The spell had been cast! The search was on for ideas for a further two tiles to be worked as companion pieces to the Turkish Tulip Tile. Sixteenth and seventeenth century enamelled wall-tiles from Persia and Syria proved to be the source and these now form the themes of the second and third parts of the book—the Persian Peony Tile and Syrian Pomegranate Tile respectively. The panels were worked on ivory silk in the rich reds, blues and greens of the original tiles, with the addition of a variety of gold metallic threads and beads.

A request to design slightly smaller and simpler embroideries lead to the challenge of taking an individual motif from the three tiles and using it as the starting point for a smaller project. The brief was that the size and colours of the motif could change but the techniques should remain the same. This has been an absorbing exercise, allowing for much perusing through the vast repertoire of Islamic art—textiles, pottery, metalwork, woodwork, paintings, manuscripts and jewellery—ceramic tiles are but the tip of the

Border of ceramic tiles; Turkey (probably Iznik), sixteenth century

iceberg! The fruits of this challenge are the nine smaller embroideries featured in the first three sections of this book.

The fourth section, Miscellanea, is a diverse collection of embroideries inspired by a variety of objects—Ottoman tiles, Egyptian manuscripts, Arabian architraves, and enamelled gold vessels from Mughal India. Upon reflection, I realise that the creation of each of these pieces has been the direct result of a visit to a museum, art gallery or library—the value of exposure to the various treasures held in collections at these institutions cannot be overestimated. The images and information contained in the catalogue which accompanied the wonderful exhibition, 'The Arts of Islam', mounted at the Art Gallery of New South Wales in 2007, continues to be a valuable resource.

The delights to be found in the arts of Islam are myriad. They may be encapsulated by Herbert Cole's description of a panel of Syrian painted wall tiles, featuring stylised iris, rose and cypress tree forms, written in 1922. The colouring of the sixteenth century tiles consisted of dark and light blue (ultramarine and turquoise) and emerald greens on a white ground, with spots of decoration on the petals.

Imagine the wall spaces of a palace or mosque decorated with these wonderfully designed and coloured tiles. Think of the effect under Eastern sun-light of sapphire blue and emerald green, combined with amethyst and turquoise tints in a glazed surface, and it will not be difficult to account for the enchanted palaces covered with jewels which the romantic story-tellers of the Arabian Nights so eloquently describe.

HERBERT COLE, *Heraldry: Decoration and Floral Forms, page 189*

Glazed earthenware tile, Iran/Persia; fifteenth century

Islamic Tiles

By the eighth century, the Islamic civilisation had spread over a vast area, extending from Morocco and parts of Spain in the west to India and Uzbekistan in the east. The cultural and geographical diversity of these lands is reflected in the architecture and decorative arts—pottery, textiles, glass, woodwork, metalwork, jewellery, painting and illuminated manuscripts—that comprise the rich heritage of Islamic art.

The legacy of the Islamic potters to the world is unique. It was they who first saw the potential of white tin glaze as a 'canvas' for ceramic decoration. It was they who first used cobalt blue on that white ground, hence invented 'blue-and-white', centuries before such a colour scheme became the trademark of Chinese export porcelain and then of European taste. And it was they who developed lustre, that extraordinarily luxurious metallic sheen, which rivals precious metal in its effects, all but turning objects of clay to gold.

JAMES W. ALLAN, *Islamic Ceramics, page 3*

The splendour of Islamic tiles is legendary; the first were produced in Mesopotamia in the ninth century. The manufacture of tin-glazed pottery tiles, a characteristic feature of Near Eastern architecture, began in thirteenth century Persia, and by the sixteenth century had spread north, east and west throughout the Islamic world. They were used to embellish the interior and exterior walls, floors and ceilings of palaces, public buildings and places of worship, buildings which were largely made with brick and stone walls in an attempt to beat the heat. In a hot and dusty environment, these beautifully coloured, enamelled tiles were not only decorative but also practical and hygienic.

Produced in a variety of styles and shapes, the tiles displayed a diverse range of ornament, with geometric patterns, calligraphy (in Arabic script) and the arabesque being the characteristic elements. The arabesque, a type of vine scroll, is one of the most distinctive features of Islamic design. Based on the convolvulus (a vine with slender twining stems and trumpet-shaped flowers), it is characterised by a stem that divides regularly into a series of secondary stems, which can divide again or curve back into

It is perhaps because so much of the Near and Middle East is desert that colour becomes so important. Towns like Shiraz in south-west Iran epitomise the contrast: the bare hillsides and plains give way to pomegranate groves with their brilliant scarlet flowers, to lush gardens with flower-edged water courses, beds of roses and purple bougainvilleas, to turquoise domes and multicoloured tilework. JAMES W. ALLAN, *Islamic Ceramics, Page 4*

the main stem. Within this elegant grid, the tile painters drew stylised interpretations of the flowers inhabiting the enclosed gardens of Islam—tulips, lotus, pomegranates, lilies, iris, peonies, hyacinths, roses, carnations, cornflowers, and sprigs of prunus and fruit blossom—all intermingled with serrated saz leaves (spiky green leaves). They then painted them in beautiful vibrant colours—cobalt blue, turquoise, aquamarine, green, strong yellow, manganese purple and a brilliant coral red.

Single-colour glazed tiles were also widely used to decorate mosques and palaces from Moorish Spain to Central Asia. Cut and trimmed into squares, rectangles, hexagons, triangles and star shapes, these tiles served a function similar to that of coloured stone or marble in mosaic, and were used to create intricate geometric designs, to a degree of complexity and sophistication that had never before been seen. The panels of abstract mosaic tiles often had an upper border of calligraphic tiles, featuring the elegant decorative qualities of Arabic script. Another style of cut-tile mosaic, known as 'inlay work', blossomed during the fourteenth and fifteenth centuries. Brilliant monochrome glazed tiles—turquoise, emerald green, ultramarine, white and a reddish brown—were cut into intricate shapes and inserted into complex arabesque and floral designs, often contained within ornate borders.

We have inherited a magnificent repository of designs and colours from Islamic tile artists. From the elegant arabesques and interlacing floral motifs, to the single tiles in composite tile patterns, we have a rich resource that never ceases to fascinate and inspire.

Christopher Dresser: Decorative panel composed of Islamic arabesques.
Modern Ornamentation, 1886.

Before you begin …

The projects in this book are worked with surface embroidery, goldwork and stumpwork techniques. Before you begin, it will be helpful to read the following information:

- The diagrams at the beginning of each project are actual size, except for the Tulip Needlebook on page 47 and the Iris Book Cover on page 163. The explanatory drawings accompanying the instructions have often been enlarged for clarity.

- Read through all the instructions before commencing work on a project. As a general rule, work all surface embroidery before applying any raised or detached elements.

- Detailed instructions for the transferring of designs are provided in Part 5: Techniques, Equipment and Stitch Glossary.

- I have used Au Ver à Soie stranded silk, Soie d'Alger, for most of the embroidery. The colours I have used are from the new range of colours. Where possible, I have given DMC stranded cotton equivalents for the Soie d'Alger threads—the colours are close but not exactly the same.

- Most embroidery is worked with one strand of thread unless otherwise stipulated.

- For general information regarding techniques and equipment, please refer to Part 5: Techniques, Equipment and Stitch Glossary. If you are new to stumpwork, it is important that you read this section before undertaking any of the projects. As there is not the space here to provide detailed instructions on basic stumpwork techniques, you may like to refer to one of the stumpwork embroidery books listed in the Bibliography.

SELECT BIBLIOGRAPHY

Allan, James W.
Islamic Ceramics. Ashmolean Museum, Oxford, 1991.

Canby, Sheila R.
Islamic Art in Detail. The British Museum Press, London, 2005.

Cole, Herbert.
Heraldry: Decoration and Floral Forms. Crescent Books, New York, 1988.

Lang, Gordon.
1000 Tiles. A & C Black, London, 2004.

Rogers, J.M.
The Arts of Islam. Art Gallery NSW, Sydney, 2007.

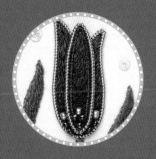

turkish

❧ TURKISH TULIP TILE DESIGNS ❧

*The tulip was loved by the Ottoman Turks and it was used
extensively to decorate silks, ceramics, metal, stone and wood.
Most favoured was the red tulip with dagger-shaped flowers tapering to
long narrow petals. This section features the Turkish Tulip Tile, an exotic
panel inspired by a sixteenth century Turkish enamelled wall tile.*

*Three smaller projects follow—Miniature Tulip Tile, Tulip Needlebook
and Iznik Carnation Tile—each designed around a single
motif from the Turkish Tulip Tile.*

Turkish Tulip Tile

This exotic panel was inspired by a sixteenth century Turkish enamelled wall tile. Combining stumpwork, goldwork and surface embroidery techniques, this ogival tile is worked on an ivory silk background with silks, gold metallic threads, beads and tiny spangles. The design features red tulips with detached petals, blue carnations and beaded prunus blossoms, and is enclosed by an ornate border worked in gold metallic threads and beads.

PAINTED ENAMELLED EARTHENWARE TILE
turkish, sixteenth century

Sixteenth century Turkish tiles, produced at Iznik in Anatolia, were characterised by the fluently drawn floral patterns featuring tulips, carnations, tapering saz leaves and meandering prunus blossoms. This image was the inspiration for the Turkish Tulip Tile.

Saz: A term originally used in fourteenth century Turkish to mean a forest; it also refers to a bamboo reed. In decoration, it is now used to describe a style characterised by long and curved serrated leaves known too as hançer. *N. Atasoy & J. Raby, Iznik, page 12.*

EMBROIDERED BOOK COVER
inspired by the drawing of the
sixteenth century Turkish tile.
Jane Nicholas, 2001.

EMBROIDERED PANEL
inspired by the drawing of the
sixteenth century Turkish tile,
inserted into the lid of a box.
Jane Nicholas, 2004.

TURKISH TULIP TILE SKELETON DIAGRAM

drawings actual size

skeleton outline

3d   4d

Detached tulip petal outlines

TURKISH TULIP TILE
❧ OVERALL REQUIREMENTS ❧

This is the complete list of requirements for this embroidery

- ✛ ivory silk background fabric: 30 cm (12 in) square
- ✛ quilter's muslin (or calico) backing fabric: 30 cm (12 in) square
- ✛ red cotton fabric (homespun): 15 cm (6 in) square
- ✛ bottle-green felt: 5 x 8 cm (2 x 3 in)
- ✛ red felt: 5 x 8 cm (2 x 3 in)
- ✛ paper-backed fusible web: 10 x 8 cm (4 x 3 in)

- ✛ 25 cm (10 in) embroidery hoop or stretcher bars
- ✛ 10 cm (4 in) embroidery hoop
- ✛ needles:

  crewel/embroidery size 10

  sharps size 12

  sharps size 9

  tapestry size 28

  sharp yarn darners sizes 14–18
- ✛ beeswax
- ✛ embroidery equipment

- ✛ green stranded thread (stems, leaves, carnations):

  Soie d'Alger 1846 or DMC 500
- ✛ blue stranded thread (carnations): Soie d'Alger 4924 or DMC 824
- ✛ red stranded thread (tulips, border): Soie d'Alger 942 or DMC 321

For ease of use, the requirements of each individual element are repeated under its heading—for example, Stems and Leaves requirements, Carnations requirements.

- ✢ Japanese gold T70
- ✢ gilt 3-ply twist
- ✢ gilt super pearl purl
- ✢ gilt no. 3 pearl purl
- ✢ fine gold metallic thread: YLI 601 Metallic Thread col. gold
- ✢ fine gold silk thread: YLI Silk Stitch 50 col. 79
- ✢ nylon clear thread: Madeira Monofil 60 col. 1001
- ✢ red sewing thread: Gutermann Polyester col. 365

- ✢ Mill Hill seed beads 00123 (cream)
- ✢ Mill Hill petite beads 40557 (gold)
- ✢ Mill Hill petite beads 40332 (green)
- ✢ Mill Hill petite beads 42028 (ginger)
- ✢ 3 mm red pearls
- ✢ 2 mm gold spangles

- ✢ 33 gauge white covered wire (tulips):
- ✢ four 12 cm (4½ in) lengths
  (colour wire red if desired, Copic R17 Lipstick Orange)

TURKISH TULIP TILE
❧ PREPARATION ❧

Mount the silk background fabric and the muslin backing
into the 25 cm (10 in) embroidery hoop or frame.

Trace the skeleton outline on to the background fabric,
taking care to align the design with the grain of the fabric
(see Techniques, Equipment and Stitch Glossary, Part 5).

Using gold silk thread in a small sharps needle, work a row
of running stitches along both border lines. As the border
threads will be applied over these running stitches, they
need to be quite small and accurate.

Stems & Leaves

REQUIREMENTS

✛ green stranded thread: Soie d'Alger 1846 or DMC 500

✛ Japanese gold T70

STEMS

Using one strand of green thread in a crewel needle, couch a double row of Japanese gold thread along all stem lines (except the prunus blossom stems which have a single row), working the stitches 2–3 mm apart. Following the recommended order of work, begin by sinking the tails of gold thread through to the back at the lower edge of the specified flower, then couch along the stem line towards the base of the design, sinking the tails of gold thread as required. Trim and secure all thread tails to the backing fabric.

1. Couch the lower carnation (1) stems, sinking the inner thread tails where the stems meet. Couch the remaining threads along the centre line until just before the junction with the tulip stems. Park the threads. Sink the tails *after* the tulip stems are worked.

2. Couch the middle carnation (2) stems, sinking the inner thread tails where the stems meet. Couch the remaining threads along the centre line, sinking the tails at the junction with the lower carnation stems.

3. Couch the upper tulip (3) stems, sinking the tails of thread under all the carnation stems (or work over them if preferred), until just before the junction with the lower tulip stems. Park the threads.

4. Couch the lower tulip (4) stems to the junction with upper tulip stems. Sink both inner thread tails and couch the remaining threads along the stem to the centre line. Couch both rows of thread, side by side along the centre line, until the lower point is reached. Sink the threads, the centre two slightly longer than the outside threads, to form a neat end.

5. Sink the lower carnation tails.

6. Couch the upper carnation (5) stem, sinking the tails where the upper tulip stems touch.

Note: Work the prunus blossom stems *after* the blossoms are applied.

LEAVES

With one strand of green thread in a crewel needle, outline the leaves in split stitch, then work a few padding stitches. Embroider each leaf in satin stitch, working the stitches at an angle across the leaf and enclosing the outline.

Note: Work the prunus blossom leaves *after* the blossoms are applied.

Carnations

REQUIREMENTS

+ bottle-green felt: 5 x 8 cm (2 x 3 in)
+ paper-backed fusible web: 5 x 8 cm (2 x 3 in)
+ green stranded thread: Soie d'Alger 1846 or DMC 500
+ blue stranded thread: Soie d'Alger 4924 or DMC 824
+ gilt super pearl purl
+ fine gold metallic thread: YL1 601 Metallic Thread col. gold
+ Fine gold silk thread: YLI Silk Stitch 50 col. 79
+ Mill Hill petite beads 40557 (gold)
+ Mill Hill petite beads 40332 (green)

PETALS

The carnation petals are worked in needle-weaving.

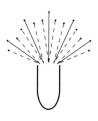

1. Using two long strands of blue thread in a crewel needle, stitch the 'spokes' for the needle-weaving as follows, securing the thread behind the carnation base as required:

• Work a straight stitch from each of the outer five dots to the points at the top of the carnation base (five separate entry points).

• Work a slightly shorter stitch on each side of these five stitches, using the same lower entry point for each pair of stitches. There will be fifteen 'spokes' in all—one long stitch and two shorter stitches for each petal.

CARNATIONS & TULIP RHODIAN DISH, SIXTEENTH CENTURY
Elegantly shaped carnations and pinks were used extensively by Turkish and Persian artists to decorate their ceramics, textiles, carpets and illuminated manuscripts.

2. With one long strand of blue thread in a tapestry needle, fill each group of three straight stitches with needle-weaving, starting at the base and working towards the top of the petal. Weave until the ends of the shorter side stitches are reached, take the thread to the centre then wrap the end of the centre stitch (approximately 4 wraps) to form a point at the end of the petal. Repeat for the remaining four petals.

CARNATION BASE

1. Trace five carnation base padding shapes (1, 2 and 5) onto paper-backed fusible web and fuse to green felt. Cut out the shapes. With one strand of green thread in a crewel needle, apply the shapes (web side down) over the base outlines on the background fabric, using small stab stitches. Make sure the felt shape is no larger than the design outline.

2. The felt base padding is outlined in gilt super pearl purl, couched in place with waxed silk thread in a small sharps needle. Starting at a top corner, couch purl around the base to the other corner. Using tweezers, bend purl into sepal points before couching in place across the top of the base. Make sure the couching stitches are pulled firmly between the coils of the purl (stretch purl slightly before couching to facilitate this).

3. With one strand of green thread in a small Sharps needle, stitch green and gold petite beads inside the purl outline to cover the carnation base. Try to stitch each bead in a different direction, and use more green beads than gold (5—6).

4. Work a detached chain stitch into the base of each petal with one strand of fine Gold Metallic thread in a size 9 Sharps needle.

Tulips

REQUIREMENTS

- ✢ red cotton fabric (homespun) : 15 cm (6 in) square
- ✢ red felt: 5 x 8 cm (2 x 3 in)
- ✢ paper-backed fusible web: 5 x 8 cm (2 x 3 in)
- ✢ red stranded thread (tulips): Soie d'Alger 942 or DMC 321
- ✢ red sewing thread: Gutermann Polyester col. 365
- ✢ gilt super pearl purl
- ✢ fine gold metallic thread: YL1 601 Metallic Thread col. gold
- ✢ fine gold silk thread: YLI Silk Stitch 50 col. 79
- ✢ nylon clear thread: Madeira Monofil 60 col. 1001
- ✢ Mill Hill petite beads 40557 (gold)
- ✢ Mill Hill petite beads 42028 (ginger)
- ✢ 33 gauge white covered wire: four 12 cm (4½ in) lengths
  (colour wire red if desired, Copic R17 Lipstick Orange)

Tulip from enamelled pottery, Turkish, sixteenth century

BACKGROUND PETALS

1. Trace the tulip padding shapes (3 and 4) to paper-backed fusible web and fuse to red felt. Cut out the shapes. With one strand of red sewing thread in a crewel needle, apply the shapes (web side down) over the outlines on the background fabric, using small stab stitches. Make sure the felt shape is no larger than the design outline.

2. Starting at the centre of the top edge, couch gilt super pearl purl around the felt tulip shape, using tweezers to bend the purl into defined points at the tips of the petals. Use waxed gold silk thread in a small sharps needle and make sure the couching stitches are pulled firmly between the coils of the purl.

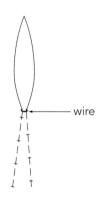

3. Embroider the felt background petal, inside the purl outline, in long and short stitch using one strand of red thread in a crewel needle.

DETACHED PETALS

1. Mount red cotton fabric into a small hoop and trace four detached tulip petals, two large (3d) for the upper tulips and two small (4d) for the lower tulips, placing the petals on the straight grain of the fabric.

2. Bend one piece of wire in half then insert both tails through to the back at the base of the petal shape. With one strand of red thread in a crewel needle, couch the wire around the petal outline, keeping the tails of wire out of the way at the back, then buttonhole stitch the wire to fabric. Embroider the petal in long and short stitch.

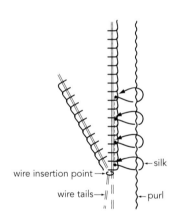

3. Using waxed gold silk thread in a small Sharps needle, couch Gilt Super Pearl Purl around the edge of the petal, starting and ending at the wire insertion point and keeping the wire tails out of the way at the back. Work the couching stitches into the buttonholed edge as follows:

- Bring the needle up between the wire and the edge of the buttonhole stitch.
- Slip the needle around the purl then go down into the same hole.
- Pull the thread firmly so that the stitches slide between the coils of the purl.
- Repeat, working the stitches about 2 mm ($^1/_{16}$ in) apart.

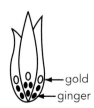

4. Carefully cut out the petal and bend slightly into a curved shape. Apply the detached petal over the embroidered lower petals by inserting the wire tails through to the back, just inside the purl outline, using a large yarn darner (check that the correct petals are applied—3d to 3 and 4d to 4). Secure the wires at the back and trim.

5. With nylon thread in a small sharps needle, stitch petite gold and ginger beads at the base of the tulip, stitching right through to the back.

Prunus Blossom

REQUIREMENTS

+ 3 mm red pearls
+ Mill Hill seed beads 00123 (cream)
+ nylon clear thread: Madeira Monofil 60 col. 1001
+ green stranded thread: Soie d'Alger 1846 or DMC 500
+ Japanese gold T70
+ fine gold metallic thread: YL1 601 Metallic Thread col. gold

1. Using nylon thread in a small sharps needle, stitch a red pearl in the centre of the blossom (4 stitches).

2. Stitch one cream seed bead next to the red pearl (the hole parallel to the edge of the red bead). Bring the needle to the front, pass it through the cream bead, then thread on eight more beads. Pass needle through the first bead again, forming a circle of cream beads.
Take the needle through to the back and bring out on the other side of the circle of beads. Couch between each cream bead, then thread the needle through all nine beads several times to pull the beads into an even circle. Secure the thread.

red bead

cream bead

3. Using one strand of green thread in a crewel needle, work the leaf stalks and outline the leaves in split stitch. Embroider the leaves in padded satin stitch.

4. With one strand of green thread, couch a single row of Japanese gold

thread along the blossom stems, sinking the tails of gold thread through to the back.

5. With one strand of fine gold metallic thread in a size 9 sharps needle, work a straight stitch between each cream bead, working the stitches towards the centre red bead.

Note: Work the prunus blossoms in the border *after* the inner line of the border is stitched.

Border & Spangles

The border is worked over the two lines of running stitch; it is not necessary to remove these stitches.

REQUIREMENTS

+ Japanese gold T70
+ gilt 3-ply twist
+ gilt no. 3 pearl purl
+ red stranded thread: Soie d'Alger 942 or DMC 321
+ fine gold metallic thread: YL1 601 Metallic Thread col. gold
+ nylon clear thread: Madeira Monofil 60 col. 1001
+ Mill Hill seed beads 00123 (cream)
+ Mill Hill petite beads 40557 (gold)
+ 3 mm red pearls
+ 2 mm gold spangles

INNER BORDER LINE

1. Leaving 5 cm (2 in) tails of thread at each end, couch a length of Japanese gold thread and a length of gilt 3-ply twist together along the inner line (Japanese gold on the inside), using waxed, fine gold metallic thread in size 9 sharps needle. Work the couching stitches 2–3 mm apart and sink the tails of gold thread after the couching is complete.

2. Work a beaded prunus blossom at the upper and lower points of the inner border line (omitting the gold straight stitches).

OUTER BORDER LINE

1. Cut a 10 cm (4 in) length of gilt no. 3 pearl purl and stretch to 18 cm (7 in) by holding a coil of purl at each end and pulling apart gently. Using six strands of red thread, carefully wrap the purl between each coil, leaving a tail of thread at each end (trim the final coil at each end to neaten, if necessary). Sink one tail of wrapping thread next to the blossom at one end of the outer line and hold at the back with masking tape. With one strand of red thread in a crewel needle, couch the wrapped purl over the line of running stitch, working the stitches at an angle over the wrapped purl, one stitch every third or fourth coil, bringing the needle up and down, 3–4 mm apart, on the line. Just before the other end of the line is reached, unwrap the red thread and cut the purl to the correct length, rewrap the end of the purl then sink the wrapping thread next to the blossom. Secure both ends of red thread at the back.

2. Couch a length of gilt 3-ply twist along the outer edge of the wrapped purl, sinking the tails close to the blossoms. Use waxed, fine gold metallic thread, working the couching stitches into the twist if preferred.

3. Using nylon thread in a small sharps needle, stitch a row of petite gold beads, 4 mm (3/16 in) apart, inside the border lines (the holes in the beads lie at right angles to the border). Starting at the centre point of one border, apply the beads up to one blossom, stitch back through these beads to the centre point, then apply the beads down to the other blossom. Stitch back through these beads to the centre point, thus making two stitches in each bead. The best result is obtained by making the first stitch through the bead quite long, using the second stitch to accurately position the bead. Work all stitches towards the outer line of the border. A paper ruler may be used, on its side, to accurately mark the position of the beads.

4. Stitch gold spangles to background with nylon or fine gold metallic thread, making three stitches into each spangle (secure the thread behind each spangle before moving on to the next one).

Miniature Tulip Tile

A tulip from the Turkish Tulip Tile forms the central motif in this elegant miniature tile. Using stumpwork, goldwork and surface embroidery techniques, the diamond-shaped panel is worked on an ivory silk background with silks, gold metallic threads, beads and tiny spangles. The design features a red tulip with a detached petal, set in an ornate border worked in gold metallic threads and beads.

This tile may be framed or made into the lid of a box.

MINIATURE TULIP TILE
❧ REQUIREMENTS ❧

This is the complete list of requirements for this embroidery

- ✛ ivory silk background fabric: 20 cm (8 in) square
- ✛ quilter's muslin (or calico) backing fabric: 20 cm (8 in) square
- ✛ red cotton fabric (homespun) : 15 cm (6 in) square
- ✛ red felt: 5 x 8 cm (2 x 3 in)
- ✛ paper-backed fusible web: 5 x 8 cm (2 x 3 in)

- ✛ 15 cm (6 in) embroidery hoop
- ✛ 10 cm (4 in) embroidery hoop
- ✛ needles:

  crewel/embroidery size 10

  sharps size 12

  sharps size 9

  sharp yarn darners sizes 14–18
- ✛ beeswax
- ✛ embroidery equipment

- ✛ green stranded thread (stem, leaves) : Soie d'Alger 1846 or DMC 500
- ✛ red stranded thread (tulip, border) : Soie d'Alger 942 or DMC 321

- ✛ Japanese gold T70
- ✛ gilt 3-ply twist
- ✛ gilt super pearl purl
- ✛ gilt no. 3 pearl purl
- ✛ fine gold metallic thread: YLI 601 Metallic Thread col. gold
- ✛ fine gold silk thread: YLI Silk Stitch 50 col. 79
- ✛ nylon clear thread: Madeira Monofil 60 col. 1001
- ✛ red sewing thread: Gutermann Polyester col. 365

- ✛ Mill Hill seed beads 00123 (cream)
- ✛ Mill Hill petite beads 40557 (gold)
- ✛ Mill Hill petite beads 42028 (ginger)
- ✛ 3 mm red pearls
- ✛ 2 mm gold spangles

- ✛ 33 gauge white covered wire (tulip): 12 cm (4½ in) length
  (colour wire red if desired, Copic R17 Lipstick Orange)

MINIATURE TULIP TILE DIAGRAMS
drawings actual size

skeleton outline

Tulip padding
shape

Detached tulip
petal outline

MINIATURE TULIP TILE
❧ PREPARATION ❧

Mount the silk background fabric and the muslin
backing into the 15 cm (6 in) embroidery hoop.

Trace the skeleton outline on to the background fabric,
taking care to align the design with the grain of the fabric
(place a board underneath the hoop of
fabric to provide a firm surface).

Using gold silk thread in a small sharps needle, work a
row of running stitches along both border lines.
As the border threads will be applied over these running
stitches, they need to be quite small and accurate.

Stem

Using one strand of green thread in a crewel needle, couch a double row of Japanese gold thread along the central stem line, working the stitches 2–3 mm apart. Begin by sinking the tails of gold thread through to the back at the lower edge of the tulip, then couch along the stem line towards the base of the design, sinking the tails of thread at the end of the line. Secure the tails of thread to the backing fabric, behind the stem.

Leaves

With one strand of green thread, outline the leaves in split stitch, then work a few padding stitches. Embroider both leaves in satin stitch, working the stitches at an angle across the leaf and enclosing the outline.

Tulip

Work as for the tulip in the Turkish Tulip Tile with the following variations. For diagrams and more detailed instructions see pages 28–30.

BACKGROUND PETALS

1. Trace the tulip padding shape to paper-backed fusible web and fuse to red felt. Cut out the shape. With one strand of red sewing thread, apply the shape (web side down) over the outline on the background fabric, using small stab stitches. Make sure the felt shape is no larger than the design outline.

2. Starting at the centre of the top edge, couch gilt super pearl purl around the felt tulip shape, using tweezers to bend the purl into defined points at the tips of the petals. Use waxed gold silk thread and make sure the couching stitches are pulled firmly between the coils of the purl.

3. Embroider the felt background petal, inside the purl outline, in long and short stitch using one strand of red thread.

1. Mount red cotton fabric into a small hoop, then trace the detached tulip petal on the straight grain of the fabric.

2. Bend the length of wire in half, then insert both tails through to the back at the base of the petal shape. With one strand of red thread, couch the wire around the petal outline, keeping the tails of wire out of the way at the back, then buttonhole stitch the wire to fabric. Embroider the petal in long and short stitch.

3. Using waxed gold silk thread, couch gilt super pearl purl around the edge of the petal, starting and ending at the wire insertion point and keeping the wire tails out of the way at the back. Work the couching stitches into the buttonholed edge as follows:

- bring the needle up between the wire and the edge of the buttonhole stitch
- slip the needle around the purl then go down into the same hole
- pull the thread firmly so that the stitches slide between the coils of the purl
- repeat, working the stitches about 2 mm ($^1/_{16}$ in) apart.

4. Carefully cut out the petal and bend slightly into a curved shape. Apply the detached petal over the embroidered lower petals by inserting the wire tails through to the back, just inside the purl outline. Secure the wires at the back and trim.

5. With nylon thread, stitch petite gold and ginger beads at the base of the tulip, stitching right through to the back.

Border & Spangles

The border is worked over the two lines of running stitch (it is not necessary to remove these stitches). Work the corners first then each line of the border in the following order.

PRUNUS BLOSSOMS

Work a beaded prunus blossom at each corner of the border.

1. Using nylon thread in a small sharps needle, securely stitch a red pearl over the dots in each corner to form the centres of the blossoms.

2. To form the petals, stitch one cream bead next to the red centre bead (the hole parallel to edge of red bead). Bring the needle to the front, pass it through the cream bead, then thread on eight more cream beads. Pass needle through the first bead again, forming a circle of beads. Take the needle through to the back and bring out on the other side of the circle of beads. Couch between each cream bead, then pass the needle through all nine beads, several times, to pull into an even circle. Secure the thread. Repeat for the remaining three blossoms.

INNER BORDER LINE

Cut a 12 cm (5 in) length each of Japanese cold thread and gilt 3-ply twist. Couch the pair of threads over the inner border line between the blossoms (Japanese gold on the inside), using waxed, fine gold metallic thread in size 9 sharps needle. Work the couching stitches 2–3 mm apart and sink the tails of gold thread at the inner corners, close to the blossoms. Secure the tails. Repeat for the remaining inner border lines.

OUTER BORDER LINE

1. Cut a 10 cm (4 in) length of gilt no. 3 pearl purl and stretch to 20 cm (8 in) by holding a coil of purl at each end and pulling apart gently. Cut the expanded purl into four equal lengths (5 cm/2 in).

2. Cut a 25 cm (10 in) length of red stranded thread (remove one strand if using silk so that you have six strands).

3. Place one length of purl along an outer border line, between the beaded blossoms, and trim to the correct length. Using the six strands of red

thread, carefully wrap the purl between each coil, leaving a tail of thread
at each end. Sink one tail of wrapping thread next to the blossom at one
end of an outer border line and hold at the back with masking tape. Using
one strand of red thread in a crewel needle, couch the wrapped purl over
the outer border line, working the couching stitches at an angle over the
wrapped purl, one stitch every second or third coil, and bringing the needle
up and down on the line (2 mm apart). Just before the other blossom
is reached, check the length of the purl (stretch or unwrap and trim if
necessary), then complete the couching, sinking the tail of wrapping thread
next to the blossom. Secure both ends of wrapping thread at the back.

4. Couch a 25 cm (10 in) length of gilt 3-ply twist next to the outer edges
of the wrapped purl and around the beaded blossoms, sinking the tails at
one side (not at the edge of the blossoms). Use waxed, fine gold metallic
thread, working the couching stitches at an angle over the twist if preferred.

BEADS AND SPANGLES

1. Using nylon thread in a small sharps needle, stitch a row of petite gold
beads, 4 mm (3/16 in) apart, inside the border lines (the holes in the beads
lie at right angles to the border). Starting at the centre point of one border,
apply the beads up to one blossom, stitch back through these beads to the
centre point then apply the beads down to the other blossom. Stitch back
through these beads to the centre point, thus making two stitches in each
bead. The best result is obtained by making the first stitch through the
bead quite long, using the second stitch to accurately position the bead.
Work all stitches towards the outer line of the border. A paper ruler may be
used, on its side, to accurately mark the position of the beads.

2. Stitch gold spangles to the background with nylon or fine gold metallic
thread, making three stitches into each spangle (secure the thread behind
each spangle before moving on to the next one).

Tulip Needlebook

This elegant needlebook is based on the Miniature Tulip Tile design.

Combining goldwork and surface embroidery techniques, the

panel is worked on a dark prune-coloured silk background with silks,

gold metallic threads and beads. The design features a brick-red tulip,

set in an ornate, diamond-shaped border, surrounded by tiny gold

spangles. As this version of the tile is to be used as a needlebook, the

centre petal of the tulip has been embroidered on the silk background

rather than being detached. The design may also

be worked as a panel to be framed..

TULIP NEEDLEBOOK *showing red felt pages.*

TULIP NEEDLEBOOK DIAGRAM
enlarge 120%

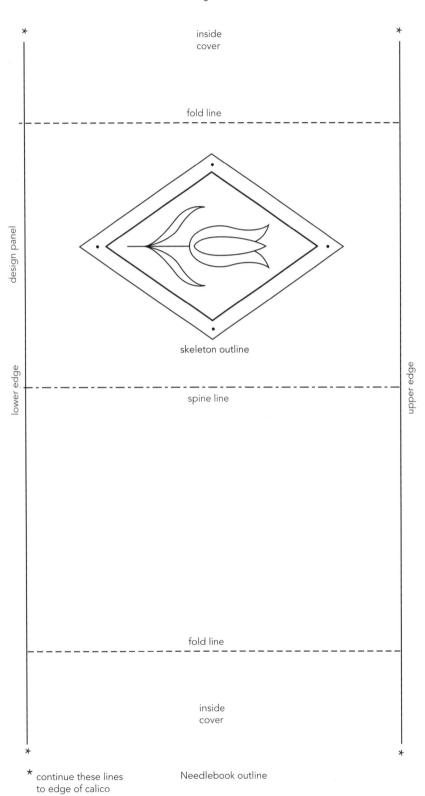

inside
cover

fold line

design panel

skeleton outline

lower edge

spine line

upper edge

fold line

inside
cover

* continue these lines
   to edge of calico

Needlebook outline

TULIP NEEDLEBOOK
❧ REQUIREMENTS ❧

This is the complete list of requirements for this embroidery

✢ prune-coloured silk background fabric: 20 x 37 cm (8 x 14½ in)

✢ calico backing fabric: 20 x 37 cm (8 x 14½ in)

✢ red felt: 5 x 8 cm (2 x 3 in)

✢ paper-backed fusible web: 5 x 8 cm (2 x 3 in)

✢ cranberry coloured felt: two pieces 12 x 18 cm (4¾ x 7 in)

✢ thin iron-on wadding (Pellon): 12 x 18 cm (4¾ x 7 in)

✢ thin card (1 mm): 12 x 18 cm (4¾ x 7 in)

....

✢ 15 cm (6 in) embroidery hoop

✢ needles:

crewel/embroidery size 10

sharps size 12

sharps size 9

sharp yarn darners sizes 14–18

✢ beeswax

- ✝ embroidery equipment
- ✝ olive-gold stranded thread (leaves): Soie d'Alger 3546
- ✝ brick-red stranded thread (tulip): Soie d'Alger 2645
- ✝ prune-coloured stranded thread (stem, border): Soie d'Alger 5116

- ✝ Japanese gold T70
- ✝ gilt 3-ply twist
- ✝ gilt super pearl purl
- ✝ gilt no. 3 pearl purl
- ✝ fine gold metallic thread: YLI 601 Metallic Thread col. gold
- ✝ fine gold silk thread: YLI Silk Stitch 50 col. 79
- ✝ nylon clear thread: Madeira Monofil 60 col. 1001
- ✝ red sewing thread: Gutermann Polyester col. 365
- ✝ purple sewing thread: Gutermann Polyester col. 512

- ✝ Mill Hill seed beads 3038 (ginger)
- ✝ Mill Hill petite beads 40557 (gold)
- ✝ Mill Hill petite beads 42028 (ginger)
- ✝ 3 mm gold pearls
- ✝ 2 mm gold spangles

TULIP NEEDLEBOOK
❧ PREPARATION ❧

Place the calico rectangle on top of the silk rectangle and secure to a table top with pieces of masking tape. With a fine lead pencil and ruler, draw a vertical line on the calico, halfway across the rectangle (spine line). Using the spine line as a guide, draw the needlebook outline and fold lines onto the calico with lead pencil, extending the upper and lower lines to the side edges. Using silk tacking thread in a small sharps needle, work a row of small running stitches along the spine line, fold lines and needlebook outline (stitching through the calico and silk). Note that the design panel is on the left of the spine line.

Mount the silk and calico 'sandwich' into the 15 cm (6 in) embroidery hoop (silk side uppermost), with the design panel in the centre of the hoop. Check that the rectangular shape of the design panel has not been distorted.

Trace the design outline on to the calico backing, taking care to align the design within the design panel outline.

Using silk tacking thread, transfer the design outline to the front (silk) by working a row of small running stitches along all design lines. Remove these stitches as the design is worked.

Stem

Using one strand of prune-coloured thread in a crewel needle, couch a double row of Japanese gold thread along the central stem line, working the stitches 2–3 mm apart. Begin by sinking the tails of gold thread through to the back at the lower edge of the tulip, then couch along the stem line towards the base of the design, sinking the tails of thread at the end of the line. Secure the tails to the backing fabric, behind the stem.

Leaves

With one strand of olive-gold thread, outline the leaves in split stitch, then work a few padding stitches. Embroider both leaves in satin stitch, working the stitches at an angle across the leaf and enclosing the outline.

Tulip

1. Trace the tulip padding shape to paper-backed fusible web and fuse to red felt. Cut out the shape. With one strand of red sewing thread in a crewel needle, apply the shape (web side down) over the outline on the background fabric, using small stab stitches. Make sure the felt shape is no larger than the design outline.

Tulip padding shape (actual size)

2. Using waxed gold silk thread in a small sharps needle, couch gilt super pearl purl around the tulip centre petal outline, using the diagram as a guide to placement. Start couching at the lower edge of the centre petal and use tweezers to bend the purl into a point at the tip of the petal. Make sure the couching stitches are pulled firmly between the coils of the purl.

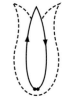

3. Starting at one edge of the centre petal, couch gilt super pearl purl around the felt tulip shape, using tweezers to bend the purl into defined points at the tips of the side petals.

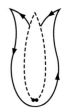

4. Embroider the tulip petals, inside the purl outlines, in long and short stitch using one strand of brick-red thread in a crewel needle.

5. With nylon thread in a small sharps needle, stitch petite gold and ginger beads at the base of the tulip, taking the stitches through to the back.

Border & Spangles

The border is worked over the two lines of running stitch—it is not necessary to remove these stitches. Work the corners first then each line of the border in the following order.

PRUNUS BLOSSOMS

Work a beaded prunus blossom at each corner of the border.

1. Using nylon thread in a small sharps needle, securely stitch a gold pearl over the dots in each corner to form the centres of the blossoms.

2. To form the blossom petals, stitch one ginger bead next to the gold centre bead (with the hole parallel to edge of gold bead). Bring the needle to the front, pass it through the ginger bead, then thread on eight more ginger beads. Pass needle through the first bead again, forming a circle of beads. Take the needle through to the back and bring out on the other side of the circle of beads. Couch between each ginger bead, then pass the needle through all nine beads, several times, to pull into an even circle. Secure the thread. Repeat for the remaining three blossoms.

INNER BORDER LINE

Cut a 12 cm (5 in) length each of Japanese gold thread and gilt 3-ply twist. Couch the pair of threads over the inner border line between the blossoms (Japanese gold on the inside), using waxed, fine gold metallic thread in size 9 sharps needle. Work the couching stitches 2–3 mm apart and sink the tails of gold thread at the inner corners, close to the blossoms. Secure the tails. Repeat for the remaining inner border lines.

OUTER BORDER LINE

1. Cut a 10 cm (4 in) length of gilt no. 3 pearl purl and stretch to 20 cm (8 in) by holding the coil of purl at each end and pulling apart gently. Cut the expanded purl into four equal lengths of 5 cm (2 in). Cut a 25 cm (10 in) length of prune-coloured stranded thread.

2. Place one length of purl along an outer border line, between the beaded blossoms, and trim to the correct length. Using six strands of prune-coloured thread, carefully wrap the purl between each coil, leaving a tail of thread at each end. Sink one tail of wrapping thread next to the blossom at one end of an outer border line and hold at the back with masking tape. Using one strand of prune-coloured thread in a crewel needle, couch the wrapped purl over the outer border line, working the couching stitches at an angle over the wrapped purl, one stitch every second or third coil, and bringing the needle up and down on the line (2 mm apart). Just before the other blossom is reached, check the length of the purl (stretch or unwrap and trim if necessary), then complete the couching, sinking the tail of wrapping thread next to the blossom. Secure both ends of wrapping thread at the back.

3. Couch a length of gilt super pearl purl next to the outer edges of the wrapped purl and around the beaded blossoms, starting and ending on one side (the cut ends of the purl abut). Use waxed, gold silk thread, making sure the couching stitches are pulled firmly between the coils of the purl.

BEADS AND SPANGLES

1. Using nylon thread in a small sharps needle, stitch a row of petite gold beads, 4 mm (3/16 in) apart, inside the border lines (the holes in the beads lie at right angles to the border). Starting at the centre point of one border, apply the beads up to one blossom, stitch back through these beads to the centre point, then apply the beads down to the other blossom. Stitch back through these beads to the centre point, thus making two stitches in each bead. The best result is obtained by making the first stitch through the bead quite long, using the second stitch to accurately position the bead. Work all stitches towards the outer line of the border. A paper ruler may be used, on its side, to accurately mark the position of the beads.

2. Stitch gold spangles to the background with fine gold metallic thread, making three stitches into each spangle (secure the thread behind each spangle before moving on to the next one). The spangles may be stitched either inside or outside the border as desired (if outside the border, make sure that they do not encroach into the seam allowance).

To complete the Needlebook

1. Remove the fabrics from the hoop and press the edges carefully on the calico side. Check the original needlebook outlines and redraw if necessary. Draw vertical lines, 17.8 cm (7 in) from the spine line, for the side edges of the needlebook.

2. Cut the calico (and the silk) along the upper, lower and side edges of the needlebook. To reduce bulk, cut the calico away from the inside covers of the needlebook, cutting close to the line of running stitches along the fold lines (retain the running stitches at this stage).

3. Press under a 1 cm (1/2 in) turning at each side edge of the silk.

4. With right sides facing, fold the front and back inside covers along the fold lines (the inside edges of the covers meet along the spine line). With right sides facing, fold both inside covers along the fold lines, with the edges of the turnings touching each other and the spine line. Pin the raw edges together across the top and bottom of the needlebook. With the calico side up, stitch a 1 cm (1/2 in) seam across the upper and lower edges of the needlebook, either by machine or by hand (back stitch) using purple sewing thread. Cut the calico seam allowance away, close to the stitching. Trim one of the silk seam allowances to 5 mm (1/4 in).

5. Turn the needlebook right side out, carefully easing out the corners. Finger-press the seam allowance. Remove any silk running stitches that remain.

6. Fuse the pellon to the thin card, then cut two shapes, each 10 x 7.5 cm (4 x 3 in).

7. Carefully ease the padded boards inside the covers of the needlebook through the opening at the spine line (padded side out); there should be an unpadded section along the spine of the needlebook to allow the covers to close easily. Close the opening at the spine line with slip stitches.

8. To prepare the pages for the needlebook, fold the strips of felt in half and place inside the padded covers. Check for size and trim to be slightly smaller than the covers (use pinking shears if desired). Back stitch (or machine stitch) all layers together along the spine line with purple thread.

Iznik Carnation Tile

The colours and design of this small square tile were

inspired by sixteenth century ceramics from Iznik, the centre of

pottery production in Ottoman Turkey. Worked in characteristic

cobalt blue and turquoise, this panel features the carnations from the

Turkish Tulip Tile, and is worked on an ivory satin background with

cottons, gold metallic threads, beads and tiny spangles. The tile

may be framed or made into the lid of a box.

IZNIK CARNATION TILE
❈ REQUIREMENTS ❈

This is the complete list of requirements for this embroidery

✛ ivory satin background fabric: 20 cm (8 in) square
✛ quilter's muslin backing fabric: 20 cm (8 in) square
✛ blue felt: 5 x 8 cm (2 x 3 in)
✛ paper-backed fusible web: 5 x 8 cm (2 x 3 in)

✛ 15 cm (6 in) embroidery hoop
✛ needles:
✛ crewel/embroidery size 10
✛ sharps sizes 9 and 12
✛ tapestry size 28
✛ sharp yarn darners sizes 14–18
✛ beeswax
✛ embroidery equipment

✛ dark cobalt blue stranded thread (stems, border): DMC 820
✛ medium cobalt blue stranded thread (leaves): DMC 796
✛ turquoise stranded thread (carnations): DMC 3844
✛ teal blue stranded thread (border): DMC 995

- ✛ teal blue cotton perle 3 thread (border):
  DMC Perle 3 col. 995
- ✛ variegated cobalt-teal viscose gimp (border): Stef Francis
  Viscose Gimp col. 23 or substitute DMC Perle 3 col. 820
- ✛ Japanese gold T70
- ✛ gilt super pearl purl
- ✛ gilt no. 2 pearl purl
- ✛ gilt milliary
- ✛ fine gold metallic thread: YLI 601 Metallic Thread col. gold
- ✛ fine gold silk thread: YLI Silk Stitch 50 col. 79
- ✛ nylon clear thread: Madeira Monofil 60 col. 1001

- ✛ Mill Hill seed beads 02089 (turquoise)
- ✛ Mill Hill petite beads 40020 (cobalt)
- ✛ 2.5 mm gold beads
- ✛ 3 mm gold beads
- ✛ 2 mm gold spangles

IZNIK CARNATION TILE DIAGRAM

drawing actual size

skeleton outline

IZNIK CARNATION TILE
❦ PREPARATION ❦

Mount the satin background fabric and the muslin
backing into the embroidery hoop.

Trace the skeleton outline on to the background fabric (see Part 5:
Techniques, Equipment and Stitch Glossary), taking care to align
the border lines with the straight grain of the fabric. Note: When
marking the points for the carnation petals, make a tiny pencil dot,
or insert a needle at each point and mark with a tacking stitch once
the tracing paper has been removed.

Using gold silk thread in a small sharps needle, work a
row of running stitches along the border line. As the border threads
will be applied over these running stitches, they
need to be quite small and accurate.

Carnations

Work as for the carnations in the Turkish Tulip Tile with the following variations. For diagrams and more detailed instructions see pages 26–28.

CARNATION PETALS

Work following the instructions for the carnation petals in the Turkish Tulip Tile, using turquoise thread instead of blue.

The carnation petals are worked in needle-weaving.

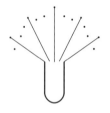

1. Using two long strands of turquoise thread in a crewel needle, stitch the 'spokes' for the needle-weaving as follows, securing the thread behind the carnation base as required.

• Work a straight stitch from each of the outer five dots to the points at the top of the carnation base (five separate entry points).

• Work a slightly shorter stitch on each side of these five stitches, using the same lower entry point for each pair of stitches. There will be fifteen 'spokes' in all—one long stitch and two shorter stitches for each petal.

2. With one long strand of turquoise thread in a tapestry needle, fill each group of three straight stitches with needle-weaving, starting at the base and working towards the top of the petal. Weave until the ends of the shorter side stitches are reached, take the thread to the centre then wrap the end of the centre stitch (approximately 4 wraps) to form a point at the end of the petal. Repeat for the remaining four petals.

CARNATION BASE

1. Trace three carnation base padding shapes onto paper-backed fusible web and fuse to blue felt. Cut out the shapes. With one strand of dark cobalt thread, apply the shapes (web side down) over the base outlines on the background fabric, using small stab stitches. Make sure the felt shape is no larger than the design outline.

2. The felt base padding is outlined in gilt super pearl purl, couched in place with waxed silk thread. Starting at a top corner, couch purl around the base to the other corner. Using tweezers, bend purl into sepal points before couching in place across the top of the base. Make sure the couching stitches are pulled firmly between the coils of the purl (stretch purl slightly before couching to facilitate this).

3. With one strand of dark cobalt thread, stitch cobalt petite beads inside the purl outline to cover the carnation base. Try to stitch each bead in a different direction.

4. Work a detached chain stitch into the base of each petal with one strand of fine gold metallic thread in a size 9 sharps needle.

Stems

Using one strand of dark cobalt thread in a crewel needle, couch a double row of Japanese gold thread along the carnation stem lines, working the centre stem first and making the stitches 2–3 mm apart. Begin by sinking the tails of gold thread through to the back at the lower edge of the carnation base, then couch along the stem line towards the base of the design, sinking the tails of gold thread as required. Secure all tails of thread at the back.
Note: Work the prunus blossom stems after the blossoms are applied.

Leaves

With one strand of medium cobalt thread in a crewel needle, outline the leaves in split stitch, then work a few padding stitches. Embroider each leaf in satin stitch, working the stitches at an angle across the leaf and enclosing the outline.
Note: Work the prunus blossom leaves after the blossoms are applied.

Prunus Blossoms

Work as for the prunus blossoms in the Turkish Tulip Tile with the following variations.

1. Using nylon thread, stitch a 2.5 mm gold bead in the centre of the blossom (4 stitches).

2. Stitch one turquoise seed bead next to the gold bead (with the hole parallel to the edge of the gold bead). Bring the needle to the front, pass it through the turquoise bead, then thread on seven more beads. Pass needle through the first bead again, forming a circle of turquoise beads. Take the needle through to the back and bring out on the other side of the circle of

beads. Couch between each turquoise bead, then thread the needle through all eight beads several times to pull the beads into an even circle. Secure the thread.

3. Using one strand of medium cobalt thread, work the leaf stalks and outline the leaves in split stitch. Embroider the leaves in padded satin stitch.

4. With one strand of dark cobalt thread, couch a single row of Japanese gold thread along the blossom stems, sinking the tails of gold thread through to the back.

5. With one strand of fine gold metallic thread in a size 9 sharps needle, work a straight stitch between each turquoise bead, working the stitches towards the centre gold bead.

Border & Spangles

Five rows of assorted threads and wires are couched side by side to produce a narrow solid border, using the outline of running stitch as a guide to placement. A 3 mm gold bead is stitched at each corner. Starting from the inside border line (1), work the border in the following order:

Row A: couched Japanese gold thread.

Row B: couched teal blue perle thread.

Row C: couched variegated viscose gimp (or cobalt perle thread).

Row D: couched cobalt-wrapped pearl purl.

Row E: couched gilt milliary.

1. COUCHED JAPANESE GOLD THREAD (ROW A)

Using nylon thread in a small Sharps needle (or fine gold metallic thread in a size 9 Sharps needle), couch a length of Japanese gold thread over the line of running stitch to form the inside row of the border. Work the stitches 2—3 mm apart and sink the tails of Japanese Gold thread through to the back at one corner. Secure and trim.

2. COUCHED TEAL BLUE PERLE THREAD (ROW B)

Using one strand of teal blue stranded thread, couch a row of teal blue Perle thread next to the row of couched gold thread, working the couching stitches towards and slightly under the Japanese gold, 2–3 mm apart, and in a brick pattern. Insert the tails of Perle thread through to the back at a different corner and secure.

3. BEADED CORNERS

Using waxed, fine gold thread in a Size 9 Sharps needle, stitch a 3 mm gold bead to each corner of the border, working the stitches towards the teal blue perle thread.

4. VARIEGATED COBALT-TEAL VISCOSE GIMP (ROW C)

Using one strand of dark cobalt stranded thread, couch a row of cobalt-teal gimp next to the row of couched perle thread, working the couching stitches towards and slightly under the perle, 2—3 mm apart, and in a brick pattern. Using a Yarn Darner, insert the tails of gimp through to the back, close to the corner beads, and secure. Work the remaining three sides of the border in the same way. DMC Perle 3 col. 820 may be substituted if the gimp is not available.

5. COBALT-WRAPPED PEARL PURL (ROW D)

• Cut a 15 cm (6 in) length of Gilt No.2 Pearl Purl and stretch to 30 cm (12 in) by holding a coil of purl at each end and pulling apart gently. Cut the stretched purl into four lengths, each 6 cm (2½ in) long (one for each side of the border). Check that the purl will fit between the beads at the corners—trim or stretch if necessary.

• Using six strands of dark cobalt thread (20 cm / 8 in length), carefully wrap the extended purl between each coil, leaving a tail of thread at each end.

• Use one strand of dark cobalt thread in a Crewel needle to couch the wrapped purl next to the row of gimp. To start, sink the tails of wrapping thread close to the corner beads (hold at the back with masking tape), then work the couching stitches at an angle over the wrapped purl, stitching towards the gimp, one stitch every second or third coil. Secure the tails of wrapping thread and trim. Work the remaining three sides of the border in the same way.

6. GILT MILLIARY (ROW E)

Using nylon thread (or fine gold metallic thread), couch a row of Gilt Milliary around the outside edge of the tile, working the couching stitches towards the wrapped purl and carefully bending the milliary at each corner to enclose the gold beads. Start and end the milliary, tails abutting, on one side of the border (not at a corner).

7. GOLD SPANGLES

Stitch gold spangles to the background with nylon or fine gold metallic thread, making three stitches into each spangle.

Panel of fritware tiles depicting a row of niches containing vases of flowers; Turkish (probably Iznik), seventeenth century

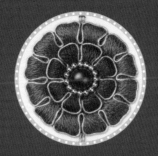

persian

With the re-opening of the Silk Route in the 1270s,
chinoiserie designs, including peonies and lotuses, passed into
Persian art. Elaborately formalised and embellished versions of peonies and
roses were used extensively by Persian artists to decorate ceramics, textiles
and carpets. This section features the Persian Peony Tile,
an elegant panel inspired by a sixteenth century Persian enamelled
wall-tile. Three smaller projects follow—Crimson Peony Rosette,
Turquoise Peony Tile and Knapweed Roundel—each designed
around a single motif from the Persian Peony Tile.

Persian Peony Tile

This elegant panel was inspired by a sixteenth century

Persian enamelled wall-tile. Combining stumpwork, goldwork and

surface embroidery techniques, the ogival tile is worked on an ivory

silk background with silks, gold metallic threads, beads and tiny

spangles. The design features a stylised peony flower, peony buds

with detached petals, feathery cobalt knapweed and beaded prunus

blossoms, and is enclosed by an ornate border worked in

gold metallic threads and beads.

PAINTED GLAZED EARTHENWARE TILES
from the bath of the Mosque of Eyub, Constantinople
Turkish, sixteenth century

The manufacture of the beautifully coloured, tin-glazed wall-tiles, which are
so characteristic of Islamic architecture, started in Persia in the thirteenth century.
This image was the inspiration for the Persian Peony Tile.

Tin-Glaze 'A lead-glaze to which a large proportion of tin oxide has been added,
making the glaze white and opaque.' *G. Lang, 1000 Tiles, page 315*

PERSIAN PEONY TILE DIAGRAMS
drawing actual size

Peony lower
petal padding

Peony upper
petal padding

Peony bud side
petal padding

Detached Peony
bud petal

Peony centre template
shape (cut from card)

PERSIAN PEONY TILE
❧ REQUIREMENTS ❧

This is the complete list of requirements for this embroidery

+ ivory silk background fabric: 30 cm (12 in) square
+ quilter's muslin (or calico) backing fabric: 30 cm (12 in) square
+ red cotton fabric (homespun): 15 cm (6 in) square
+ bottle-green felt: 5 x 8 cm (2 x 3 in)
+ red felt: 10 x 8 cm (4 x 3 in)
+ paper-backed fusible web: 15 x 8 cm (6 x 3 in)

+ 25 cm (10 in)embroidery hoop or stretcher bars
+ 10 cm (4 in)embroidery hoop
+ needles:
  crewel/embroidery size 10
  sharps size 9 and 12
  beading size 13
  sharp yarn darners sizes 14–18
+ beeswax
+ embroidery equipment

+ green stranded thread (stems, leaves, knapweed):
  Soie d'Alger 1826 or DMC 500
+ dark crimson stranded thread (peony): Soie d'Alger 2935 or DMC 326
+ medium crimson stranded thread (peony): Soie d'Alger 2934 or DMC 309
+ purple fine stranded thread (knapweed): Cifonda Art Silk 754
+ dark purple stranded thread (border): DMC 791

For ease of use, the requirements of each individual element are repeated under its heading—for example, Stems and Leaves requirements, Peony requirements.

+ Japanese gold T70
+ gilt 3-ply twist
+ gilt no. 6 smooth passing thread
+ gilt no. 2 pearl purl
+ fine gold metallic thread: YLI 601 Metallic Thread col. gold
+ fine gold silk thread: YLI Silk Stitch 50 col. 79
+ nylon clear thread: Madeira Monofil 60 col. 1001
+ red sewing thread: Gutermann Polyester col. 365

+ Mill Hill seed beads 00123 (cream)
+ 2.5 mm gold beads
+ 2 mm gold beads
+ 1.5 mm gold beads
+ 6 mm crimson pearl bead
+ 2 mm gold spangles

+ 33 gauge white covered wire: three 10 cm (4 in) lengths
  (colour wire red if desired, Copic R17 Lipstick Orange)
+ thin card for centre template

PERSIAN PEONY TILE
❧ PREPARATION ❧

Mount the silk background fabric and the muslin backing
into the 25 cm (10 in) embroidery hoop or frame.

Trace the skeleton outline on to the background fabric,
taking care to align the design with the grain of the fabric
(see Part 5: Techniques, Equipment and Stitch Glossary).

Using gold silk thread in a small sharps needle,
work a row of running stitches along both border lines,
working a back stitch into each corner of the scallops to
facilitate the working of the border. As the border
threads will be applied over these running stitches,
they need to be quite small and accurate.

Stems & Leaves

REQUIREMENTS

✢ green stranded thread: Soie d'Alger 1826 or DMC 500

✢ Japanese gold T70

Follow the recommended order of work when embroidering the stems and leaves.

STEMS

Using one strand of green thread in a crewel needle, couch a double row of Japanese gold thread along all stem lines (except the lower knapweed and prunus blossom stems which have a single row), working the stitches 2–3 mm apart and sinking the tails of gold thread as required. Trim and secure all thread tails to the backing fabric.

LEAVES

With one strand of green thread in a crewel needle, outline the leaves in split stitch then work padding stitches with chain stitch or straight stitches. Embroider each leaf with satin stitch, working the stitches at an angle across the leaf and enclosing the outline.

ORDER OF WORK

1. The teardrop shape of the peony stems is worked as a continuous line to ensure a smooth curve at the lower point. Cut two lengths of Japanese gold and gently fold in half. Couch the threads, at the fold, to the lower point of the stem line (work a stitch over each thread then one stitch over both for the neatest point), then couch the pairs of threads along the peony stem lines until just before they merge into a single stem (just below the peony flower). Sink the inner thread tails where the stems meet and couch the two outer threads along the centre stem, sinking the tails at the lower edge of the peony flower (a).

2. Embroider the two lower leaves (1), working the outline and the satin stitch over the peony flower stems. Use chain stitches to build up the leaf padding on either side of the stem to ensure a smooth surface for the satin stitch.

3. Embroider both the middle knapweed leaves (2).

4. Work the side peony bud stems, sinking the tails of gold thread at the base of the buds (b) before commencing the couching. Working towards the base, couch the threads over the embroidered leaves (2), the knapweed base outlines and the peony flower stems, leaving the tails of gold thread on the surface just before the V formed by the leaves (1). When both stems are couched, sink the outer tails of gold thread to form a V inside the embroidered leaves then sink both the inner tails.

5. Embroider leaves (3), working over the peony flower stems.

6. Work the upper knapweed stems, sinking the tails of thread at the base of the knapweed (c) before commencing the couching. Couch the threads along the stem line, sinking the gold threads on either side of the peony buds and working over the peony flower stems, leaving the tails of gold thread on the surface just before the V formed by the leaves (3). When both stems are couched, sink the tails to form a V inside the embroidered leaves, as for the peony bud stems.

7. Work the upper peony bud stem (d).

8. Embroider the remaining leaves.

9. Couch a single row of gold thread to form the lower knapweed stems (e).
Note: Work the prunus blossom stems after the blossoms are applied.

Peony

REQUIREMENTS

+ red cotton fabric (homespun): 15 cm (6 in) square
+ red felt: 10 cm x 8 cm (4 x 3 in)
+ paper-backed fusible web: 10 cm x 8 cm (4 x 3 in)
+ dark crimson stranded thread: Soie d'Alger 2935 or DMC 326
+ medium crimson stranded thread: Soie d'Alger 2934 or DMC 309
+ green stranded thread: Soie d'Alger 1826 or DMC 500
+ gilt no. 6 smooth passing
+ nylon clear thread: Madeira Monofil 60 col. 1001
+ red sewing thread: Gutermann Polyester col. 365
+ 1.5 mm gold beads
+ 6 mm crimson pearl bead
+ 33 gauge white covered wire: three 10 cm (4 in) lengths
  (colour wire red if desired, Copic R17 Lipstick Orange)
+ thin card for centre template

PETAL SHAPES

Trace the upper and lower petal shapes onto paper-backed fusible web and
fuse to red felt. Carefully cut out the upper petal shape and the lower petal
shape (also cut out the hole in the centre). Note: Do not snip too far into the
felt at the indentations separating the petals, as these need to be stitched.

LOWER PETALS

1. Using red sewing thread in a small sharps needle, apply the lower petal
shape (web side down) over the traced outline on the background fabric with
small stab stitches. First make a stitch at every petal indentation to position
the shape, then work small, close (1–1.5 mm apart) stab stitches all the way
around the outside edge (do not stitch around the centre hole).

2. With one strand of dark crimson thread in a crewel needle, make a
long straight stitch at each petal indentation to delineate the lower petals,
working from the outside edge towards the centre. Use the diagram on the
skeleton outline as a guide to length, approximately 5 mm (⅜ in), and
placement.

Floral design on an enamelled earthenware tile, reproduced by William de Morgan from a Syrian original of the sixteenth or seventeenth century

UPPER PETALS

1. Apply the upper petal shape over the lower petal shape (web side down) checking that it is centred. With red sewing thread, work a stab stitch at each petal indentation, then all the way around the outside edge.

2. Cut a circle of thin card the size of the centre template diagram and stitch it in the centre of the petal shapes with large temporary stitches (leave in place until the gilt petal edging is applied). Using red sewing thread, work a row of small back stitches around the card circle, taking the needle through all layers of fabric.

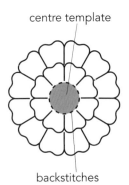

centre template

backstitches

3. With dark crimson thread, make a long straight stitch at each indentation to delineate the upper petals, working from the outside edge of the shape to the edge of the card circle.

4. With nylon thread in a small sharps needle, couch gilt smooth passing thread around the edge of each petal on the upper layer of felt. Start by inserting the tail of gilt thread at the base of one straight stitch (next to the card circle), then couch the thread around the edge of each petal shape, using the long straight stitches as a guide to the petal divisions. A loop of gilt thread, which touches the edge of the card circle, will be formed between each petal (over each straight stitch). The loops may be manipulated with tweezers to help shape the petals. Sink the remaining tail of thread when the last petal is outlined (next to the starting point). Cut the temporary threads and remove the card template.

5. With dark crimson thread in a crewel needle, embroider the upper layer of petals in satin stitch, working some shorter stitches when necessary. Work the satin stitches from the centre circle towards the edge, inserting the needle under the gilt outline.

Rose from an enamelled tile; Turkish, sixteenth century

6. Couch gilt smooth passing thread around the lower petals in the same way, using the gilt edge of the upper petals as the inner edge for the loops. Embroider the petals in satin stitch, inside the gilt outline as above, with medium crimson thread.

PEONY CENTRE

1. To make a 'hole' for the large centre bead, carefully cut a circle out of the top layer of felt, 1 mm inside the back stitch circle. Using nylon thread in a small sharps needle, stitch the 6 mm crimson pearl into the centre 'hole' with about 4 stitches (so the bead is stable).

2. Using nylon thread in a small sharps (or beading) needle, stitch a circle of small (1.5 mm) gold beads around

the centre bead as follows. Stitch one gold bead next to the centre bead (with the hole parallel to the edge of the centre bead), thread on enough gold beads to make a circle (14–15), then take the thread back through the first bead. Couch between every bead to hold the circle in place, then take the needle through all of the gold beads (like threading a necklace), several times to pull the beads into an even circle. Secure the thread.

3. With a board underneath for support, carefully shape the gilt passing around the petals into a pleasing outline, using a mellor or metal nailfile (being metal, the passing can be manipulated a little).

Peony Buds

BACKGROUND PETALS

1. Using one strand of medium crimson thread in a crewel needle, outline the three upper background petals in split stitch, working two long stitches to delineate the petals. Work padding stitches inside the outline.

2. Trace three pairs of side petals on to paper-backed fusible web (one pair for each bud), fuse to red felt and cut out. Using red sewing thread, apply the petal shapes (web side down) over the side petal outlines on the background fabric with small close stab stitches.

3. Using nylon thread in a small sharps needle, couch a row of gilt smooth passing thread around the edges of the side petals, sinking the tails at the lower points near the stem. Leave a small space at the top of the stem to insert the detached petal.

4. Couch gilt smooth passing thread around the edges of the upper three petals, making a loop over the straight stitches to form the petal divisions. Sink the tails of gilt thread at the edges of the side petals. Using medium crimson thread, embroider the upper three petals in padded satin stitch, working the stitches towards the edge of the petals, inside the gilt outline. Embroider the space between the side petals in long and short stitch.

5. With dark crimson thread, embroider the side petals in satin stitch, working the stitches towards the outside edge, inside the gilt outline.

DETACHED PETALS

1. Mount red cotton fabric into a 10 cm (4 in) hoop and trace three detached bud petals. Using dark crimson thread, couch wire around the petal outline, leaving two wire tails at the base that touch but do not cross. Buttonhole stitch the wire to the fabric, then work a row of split stitch inside the wire. Work a few padding stitches, then embroider the petal in satin stitch.

2. With nylon thread in a small sharps needle, couch gilt smooth passing thread around the edge of the petal, leaving two thread tails at the base. Work the couching stitches into the buttonhole edge, between the wire and the ridge of the buttonhole stitches, with firm stitches, 2 mm (1/16 in) apart. Cut out the petal and shape slightly.

TO COMPLETE PEONY BUD

1. Apply a detached petal over the embroidered background petals by inserting the wire tails through to the back at the base of the bud, just above the stem, using a large yarn darner. Insert the tails of gilt thread through the same hole. Bend wire and thread tails behind the bud, secure and trim.

2. With one strand of dark green thread, work a few satin stitches over the stem, at the base of the bud, to form the peduncle (work the stitches slightly wider near the base then tapering to the stem).

Knapweed

The distinctive shapes of cornflowers and knapweeds were often incorporated into the twining arabesque outlines decorating many Islamic tiles.

REQUIREMENTS

+ bottle-green felt: 5 x 8 cm (2 x 3 in)
+ paper-backed fusible web: 5 x 8 cm (2 x 3 in)
+ green stranded thread: Soie d'Alger 1826 or DMC 500
+ purple fine stranded thread: Cifonda Art Silk 754
+ fine gold metallic thread: YLI 601 Metallic Thread col. gold

BASE OF FLOWER

1. Trace the four knapweed base shapes onto paper-backed fusible web and fuse to green felt. Cut out the shapes.

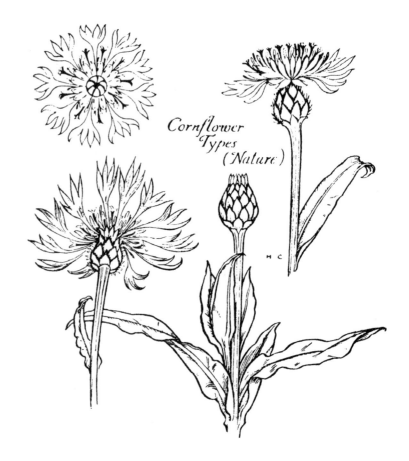

Cornflowers and knapweed

PERSIAN PEONY TILE KNAPWEED DIAGRAM   drawing actual size

2. Using dark green thread in a crewel needle, apply the felt shapes to the background (web side down) with a few stab stitches, then work a row of buttonhole stitch (stitches 1.5 mm apart) around the curved outside edge of the base (no stitches across the top V edge).

3. Cover the base in satin stitch, enclosing the buttonhole edge, and working 2–3 small stitches at each top peak.

4. With one strand of waxed fine gold metallic thread in a size 9 sharps needle, work straight stitches at an angle over the satin-stitched base (lattice couching), securing the intersections with tiny stitches also worked in the gold thread.

PETALS

The knapweed petals are worked with evenly placed straight stitches, radiating out like 'spokes' from the V at the top of the base. A fine rayon thread (e.g. Cifonda) gives the best results. Use a size 10 needle when working these stitches as the thread tends to wear in a finer needle. Keep the stitches taut and change the thread regularly to prevent 'fluffy' stitches.

1. Using tracing paper and fine needles, mark the 9 dots around the top edge of the knapweed for the petals (do not use lead pencil to mark the dots as it may show).

2. With one strand of fine purple thread in a size 10 crewel needle, work a straight stitch from each dot to the top V edge, removing the needles as you go (9 stitches), then work another stitch, the same length, between each of these stitches (8 stitches)—17 'spokes' in total.

3. Work another round of stitches between each 'spoke', 1–1.5 mm longer than the previous stitches.

4. Work 2 shorter stitches below the lower spoke on each side to complete the petals.

first round of
straight stitches

second round of
straight stitches

third round of
straight stitches

Prunus Blossom

REQUIREMENTS

✛ 2.5 mm gold beads

✛ Mill Hill seed beads 00123 (cream)

✛ nylon clear thread: Madeira Monofil 60 col. 1001

✛ green stranded thread: Soie d'Alger 1826 or DMC 500

✛ Japanese gold T70

1. Using nylon thread in a small sharps needle, securely stitch a 2.5

mm gold bead in the centre of each of the four inner blossoms. Note: the blossoms in the border have a 2 mm gold centre bead.

2. To form the petals, stitch one cream seed bead next to the gold centre bead (the hole parallel to edge of gold bead). Bring the needle to the front, pass it through the cream bead, then thread on seven more cream beads. Pass needle through the first bead again, forming a circle of beads. Take the needle through to the back and bring out on the other side of the circle of beads. Couch between each cream bead, then pass the needle through all eight beads several times to pull the beads into even circle. Secure the thread. Repeat for the other three blossoms.

3. With one strand of green thread, couch a single row of Japanese gold thread along the blossom stems, sinking the tails of gold thread through to the back.

centre
bead

Border & Spangles

REQUIREMENTS

+ Japanese gold T70
+ gilt 3-ply twist
+ gilt no.2 pearl purl
+ fine gold metallic thread: YLI 601 Metallic Thread col. gold
+ dark purple stranded thread: DMC 791
+ nylon clear thread: Madeira Monofil 60 col. 1001
+ Mill Hill seed beads 00123 (cream)
+ 2.5 mm gold beads
+ 2 mm gold beads
+ 2 mm gold spangles

The border is worked over the two lines of running stitch—it is not necessary to remove these stitches.

INNER BORDER LINE

1. Couch 40 cm (16 in) lengths of Japanese gold thread and gilt 3-ply twist together over the inner line (Japanese gold on the inside), using waxed, fine

gold metallic thread in a size 9 sharps needle. Work the couching stitches 2–3 mm apart, over both threads except at the corners of the scallops, where each thread is first couched individually then a stitch is worked over both, to achieve a sharper point. Start and end the couching just before the top curve commences (just before the inner borders meet), leaving 10 cm (4 in) tails of thread at each end.

2. Keeping the tails of twist free, couch the Japanese gold around the curved ends of the border, sinking the tails at the junction with the outer border (sink the tails of twist after the border blossom has been worked).

3. Work a beaded prunus blossom in the centre of each of the curved ends of the border. Use a 2 mm gold bead for the centre of the blossom, and 7 cream seed beads for the petals around the outside edge. Sink the tails of twist at the lower edge of the blossoms and secure.

OUTER BORDER LINE

1. Using waxed fine gold metallic thread (or nylon thread), couch a 40 cm (16 in) length of Japanese gold thread on the inside edge of the line, making loops around a 2 mm gold bead at each inner scallop point as you go. The beads may be stitched in place first (with nylon thread), or as each loop is formed. Sink the tails of gold thread at the junction with the inner border.

2. Cut a 12.5 cm (5 in) length of gilt no.2 pearl purl and stretch to 30 cm (12 in) by holding a coil of purl at each end and pulling apart gently. Using six strands of dark purple thread, carefully wrap the purl between each coil, leaving a tail of thread at each end (trim the final coil at each end to neaten, if necessary).

3. Using one strand of dark purple thread in a crewel needle, couch the wrapped purl on the outside edge of the Japanese gold thread, bending into shape at the corners with tweezers. To start, sink one tail of wrapping thread at the junction with the inner border, and hold at the back with masking tape. Work the couching stitches at an angle over the wrapped purl, one stitch every third or fourth coil, bringing the needle up and down on the line (2–3 mm apart) and working a couching stitch at each corner. Just before the end of the line is reached, unwrap the purple thread, cut the purl to the correct length, rewrap the purl and couch to the end of the line, sinking the tail of wrapping thread through to the back. Secure both tails of purple thread. The remaining stretched purl will be used to form the teardrop-shaped loops at the upper and lower points of the border.

4. Using nylon thread in a small sharps needle, stitch a 2.5 mm gold bead in the V between the gold thread at the upper and lower points of the border. Cut a 2 cm (¾ in) length of the remaining stretched purl and wrap with 6 strands of dark purple thread, leaving a tail of thread at each end of the purl. Bend the wrapped purl into a tear-drop shape, threading both tails of thread into a small yarn darner. Insert the darner behind the gold bead, taking both tails of thread through to the back. Adjust the shape of the teardrop, then couch in place with nylon thread. Repeat for the lower point of the border.

5. Stitch gold spangles to the background with nylon or fine gold metallic thread, making three stitches into each spangle (secure the thread behind each spangle before moving on to the next one).

Crimson Peony Rosette

The peony from the centre of the Persian Peony Tile is here worked individually as a rosette. Using goldwork and surface embroidery techniques, the peony is worked on an ivory satin background with silks, gold metallic threads and beads. The rosette may be made into a brooch or mounted into the lid of a small box.

ROSE

Rose: in ancient Rome, roses were an obligatory decoration at ceremonies and feasts.

In heraldry, it is a conventional five-petalled flower, with sepals or barbs between the petals, sometimes with an inner circle of five or more petals. The heraldic Tudor rose was a combination of the red and white roses of Lancaster and York, and the rose remains the Royal Badge of England.

D. Ware & M. Stafford, An Illustrated Dictionary Of Ornament, Page 183

ROSETTE

Rosette: a formalised rose, with petals radiating outwards in zones from the centre, the rosette was a primitive solar symbol, and a religious and decorative motif among the peoples of ancient India, Assyria and Persia; it became a characteristic classical motif, used by the Greeks as an architectural, funerary and ceramic ornament, and by the Romans as the central motif in the panels of coffered ceilings. Rosettes have continued in use as ceiling ornaments and, carved singly on a patera, or in series, may adorn furniture and metalwork.

D. Ware & M. Stafford, An Illustrated Dictionary Of Ornament, Page 184

PATERA

Patera: a flat, circular or oval ornament, with carved decoration, often formalised
flower petals or leaves: the word is derived from the patera, a shallow saucer,
sometimes with a handle, used as a drinking and sacrificial vessel in Roman times.

D. Ware & M. Stafford, An Illustrated Dictionary Of Ornament, Page 163

CRIMSON PEONY ROSETTE
❧ REQUIREMENTS ❧

This is the complete list of requirements for this embroidery

+ ivory satin background fabric: 15 cm (6 in) square
+ quilter's muslin: 15 cm (6 in) square
+ red felt: 5 x 8 cm (2 x 3 in)
+ paper-backed fusible web: 5 x 8 cm (2 x 3 in)

+ 10 cm (4 in) embroidery hoop
+ needles:
  crewel/embroidery size 10
  sharps size 12
  beading size 13
  sharp yarn darners sizes 14–18
+ embroidery equipment

- ✛ green stranded thread (leaves): Soie d'Alger 1826 or DMC 500
- ✛ dark crimson stranded thread (peony): Soie d'Alger 2935 or DMC 326
- ✛ medium crimson stranded thread (peony): Soie d'Alger 2934 or DMC 309

- ✛ gilt no.6 smooth passing thread
- ✛ nylon clear thread: Madeira Monofil 60 col. 1001
- ✛ red sewing thread: Gutermann Polyester col. 365

- ✛ 1.5 mm gold beads
- ✛ 6 mm crimson pearl bead

- ✛ thin card for centre template

- ✛ Framecraft 32 mm round gilt brooch, gilt trinket box or rosewood bowl

CRIMSON PEONY ROSETTE *mounted into the lid of a small box.*

CRIMSON PEONY ROSETTE DIAGRAMS
drawings actual size

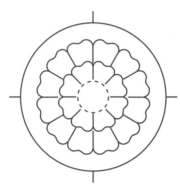

Skeleton Outline

Peony centre template
shape (cut from card)

Lower petal padding

Upper petal padding

CRIMSON PEONY ROSETTE
❦ PREPARATION ❦

Mount the satin background fabric and the muslin
backing into the 10 cm (4 in) embroidery hoop.

Trace the circle outline of the bowl or brooch onto the
backing fabric. Work a row of small running stitches
around the outline, transferring the circle to the front.

Trace the skeleton outline of the peony on to the
background fabric, inside the stitched circle outline
(place a board underneath the hoop of fabric to
provide a firm surface).

Peony

Work as for the peony flower in the Persian Peony Tile. For diagrams and more detailed instructions see pages 79–82.

Trace the upper and lower petal shapes onto paper-backed fusible web and fuse to red felt. Carefully cut out the upper petal shape and the lower petal shape (also cut out the hole in the centre). Note: Do not snip too far into the felt at the indentations separating the petals as these need to be stitched.

LOWER PETALS

1. Using red sewing thread, apply the lower petal shape (web side down) over the traced outline on the background fabric with small stab stitches. First make a stitch at every petal indentation to position the shape, then work small, close (1–1.5 mm apart) stab stitches all the way around the outside edge (do not stitch around the centre hole).

2. With one strand of dark crimson thread, make a long straight stitch at each petal indentation to delineate the lower petals, working from the outside edge towards the centre. Use the diagram on the skeleton outline as a guide to length, approximately 5 mm (⅜ in) and placement.

UPPER PETALS

1. Apply the upper petal shape over the lower petal shape (web side down), checking that it is centred. With red sewing thread, work a stab stitch at each petal indentation, then all the way around the outside edge.

2. Cut a circle of thin card the size of the centre template diagram and stitch it in the centre of the petal shapes with large temporary stitches (leave in place until the gilt petal edging is applied). Using red sewing thread, work a row of small back stitches around the card circle, taking the needle through all layers of fabric.

3. With dark crimson thread, make a long straight stitch at each indentation to delineate the upper petals, working from the outside edge of the shape to the edge of the card circle.

4. Using nylon thread, couch gilt smooth passing thread around the edge of each petal on the upper layer of felt. Start by inserting the tail of gilt thread at the base of one straight stitch (next to the card circle), then couch the thread around the edge of each petal shape, using the long straight stitches as a guide to the petal divisions. A loop of gilt thread, which touches the edge of the card circle, will be formed between each petal (over each straight stitch). The loops may be manipulated with tweezers to help shape the petals. Sink the remaining tail of thread when the last petal is outlined (next to the starting point). Cut the temporary threads and remove the card template.

5. Using dark crimson thread, embroider the upper layer of petals in satin stitch, working some shorter stitches when necessary. Work the satin stitches from the centre circle towards the edge, inserting the needle under the gilt outline.

6. Couch gilt smooth passing thread around the lower petals in the same way, using the gilt edge of the upper petals as the inner edge for the loops. Embroider the petals in satin stitch, inside the gilt outline as above, with medium crimson thread.

CENTRE

1. To make a 'hole' for the large centre bead, carefully cut a circle out of the top layer of felt, 1 mm inside the back stitch circle. Using nylon thread in a small sharps needle (or beading needle), stitch the 6 mm crimson pearl into the centre 'hole' with about 4 stitches.

2. Using nylon thread, stitch a circle of small (1.5 mm) gold beads around the centre bead as follows. Stitch one gold bead next to the centre bead (the hole parallel to the edge of the centre bead), thread on enough gold beads to make a circle (14–15), then take the thread back through first bead. Couch between every bead to hold the circle in place, then take the needle through all of the gold beads, several times, to pull the beads into an even circle. Secure the thread.

3. With a board underneath for support, carefully shape the gilt passing around the petals into a pleasing outline, using a mellor or metal nailfile (being metal, the passing can be manipulated a little).

Leaves

Using one strand of green thread, work background leaves at the junction of each petal (the leaves are optional). Each leaf is worked with five satin stitches all worked from the same point towards the peony. Check with the rim of the pot or brooch that the stitches do not extend beyond the outline.

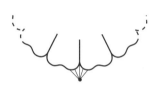

FINISHING

Mount the peony into the lid of a 32 mm round trinket box or brooch as follows:

1. Carefully trim the muslin backing to a circle slightly smaller than the circle drawn on the backing fabric.

2. Trim the satin background fabric, allowing a small seam allowance around the embroidered peony. Work a row of running stitches within the seam allowance then gather over the acetate or cardboard circle supplied, enclosing a small circle of foam (or Pellon) for padding if desired. Carefully flatten the gathers at the back with the point of an iron if necessary.

3. Insert the embroidery into the empty frame (checking that the design is centred), then push the metal plate into place as instructed.

Turquoise Peony Tile

The colours of this small square tile were inspired by a

panel of seventeenth century Persian earthenware wall tiles.

Combining goldwork and surface embroidery techniques, this panel

is worked on an olive-green silk background with silks, gold metallic

threads, beads and tiny spangles. The design features a stylised

peony flower, surrounded by a decorative border worked in

silk and metal threads, and beads. The tile may be

framed or made into the lid of a box.

TURQUOISE PEONY TILE
❦ REQUIREMENTS ❦

This is the complete list of requirements for this embroidery

✤ green silk background fabric (or colour of choice) : 20 cm (8 in) square

✤ quilter's muslin: 20 cm (8 in) square

✤ turquoise felt: 5 x 8 cm (2 x 3 in)

✤ cobalt-blue felt: 5 x 8 cm (2 x 3 in)

✤ paper-backed fusible web: 8 x 10 cm (3 x 4 in)

✤ 15 cm (6 in) embroidery hoop

✤ needles:

crewel/embroidery sizes 3—10

sharps sizes 9 and 12

beading size 13

tapestry size 28

sharp yarn darners sizes 14—18

✤ beeswax

✤ embroidery equipment

✤ turquoise stranded thread (lower petals): Soie d'Alger 135 or DMC 3809

✤ cobalt blue stranded thread (upper petals): Soie d'Alger 4916 or DMC 791

✤ burgundy stranded thread (border): Soie d'Alger 5116 or DMC 154

✤ purple cotton perle 3 thread (border): DMC Perle 3 col. 791

✤ purple stranded thread (border): DMC 791

- ✛ Japanese gold T70
- ✛ gilt 3-ply twist
- ✛ gilt no. 6 smooth passing thread
- ✛ gilt no. 3 pearl purl
- ✛ fine gold metallic thread: YLI 601 Metallic Thread col. gold
- ✛ fine gold silk thread: YLI Silk Stitch 50 col. 79
- ✛ nylon clear thread: Madeira Monofil 60 col. 1001
- ✛ turquoise and cobalt sewing thread to match felt

- ✛ Mill Hill antique beads 3025 (wildberry)
- ✛ 2.5 mm gold beads
- ✛ 1.5 mm gold beads
- ✛ 6 mm turquoise pearl bead
- ✛ 2 mm gold spangles

- ✛ 30 gauge white covered wire: twelve 12 cm (4 ¾ in) lengths
  (colour wire teal if desired, Copic BG09 Blue Green)
- ✛ thin card for centre template

TILE DIAGRAM

drawing actual size

Skeleton outline

Upper petal padding

Lower petal padding

Centre template
(cut from card

TURQUOISE PEONY TILE
❧ PREPARATION ❧

Mount the silk background fabric and the muslin backing
into the 15 cm (6 in) embroidery hoop.

Trace the skeleton outline on to the backing fabric, taking
care to align the design with the grain of the fabric.

Using gold silk thread in a small sharps needle,
work a row of running stitches along both border lines,
and the centre diagonal guide lines. As the border
threads will be applied over these running stitches,
they need to be quite small and accurate.

Peony

Work as for the peony in the Persian Peony Tile with the following variations. For diagrams and more detailed instructions see pages 79–82.

Trace the upper and lower petal padding shapes on to paper-backed fusible web. Fuse the upper peony shape to cobalt felt and the lower peony shape to turquoise felt. Carefully cut out the upper petal shape and the lower petal shape (also cut out the hole in the centre).

Note: Do not snip too far into the felt at the indentations separating the petals as these need to be stitched.

LOWER PETALS

1. Using turquoise sewing thread, apply the lower petal shape (web side down) over the traced outline on the background fabric with small stab stitches. First make a stitch at every petal indentation to position the shape, then work small, close (1–1.5 mm apart) stab stitches all the way around the outside edge (do not stitch around the centre hole).

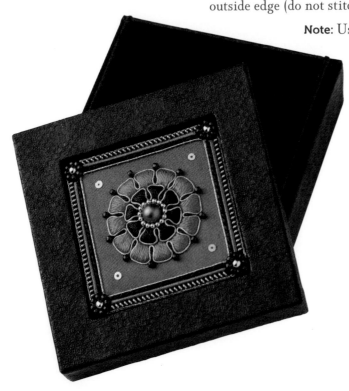

Note: Use the stitched diagonal guide lines to help with the placement of the felt shapes (remove these stitches after the felt is applied).

2. With one strand of turquoise stranded thread, make a long straight stitch at each petal indentation to delineate the lower petals, working from the outside edge towards the centre. Use the diagram on the skeleton outline as a guide to length, approximately 5 mm (⅜ in), and placement.

UPPER PETALS

1. Using cobalt sewing thread, apply the upper petal shape over the lower petal shape (web side down), checking that it is centred. Work a stab stitch at each petal indentation, then all the way around the outside edge.

2. Cut a circle of thin card the size of the centre template diagram and stitch it in the centre of the petal shapes with large temporary stitches (leave in place until the gilt petal edging is applied). Using cobalt sewing thread, work a row of small back stitches around the card circle, taking the needle through all layers of fabric.

3. With cobalt blue stranded thread, make a long straight stitch at each indentation to delineate the upper petals, working from the outside edge of the shape to the edge of the card circle.

4. With nylon thread in a small sharps needle, couch gilt smooth passing thread around the edge of each petal on the upper layer of felt. Start by inserting the tail of gilt thread at the base of one straight stitch (next to the card circle), then couch the thread around the edge of each petal shape, using the long straight stitches as a guide to the petal divisions. A loop of gilt thread, which touches the edge of the card circle, will be formed between each petal (over each straight stitch). The loops may be manipulated with tweezers to help shape the petals. Sink the remaining tail of thread when the last petal is outlined (next to the starting point). Cut the temporary threads and remove the card template.

5. With cobalt blue stranded thread, embroider the upper layer of petals in satin stitch, working some shorter stitches when necessary. Work the satin stitches from the centre circle towards the edge, inserting the needle under the gilt outline.

6. Couch gilt smooth passing thread around the lower petals in the same way, using the gilt edge of the upper petals as the inner edge for the loops. Embroider the petals in satin stitch, inside the gilt outline as above, with turquoise stranded thread.

CENTRE

1. To make a 'hole' for the large centre bead, carefully cut a circle out of the top layer of felt, 1 mm inside the back stitch circle. Using nylon thread, stitch the 6 mm turquoise pearl into the centre 'hole' with about 4 stitches.

2. Using nylon thread in a small sharps (or beading) needle, stitch a circle of small (1.5 mm) gold beads around the centre bead as follows. Stitch one gold bead next to the centre bead (the hole parallel to the edge of the centre bead), thread on enough gold beads to make a circle (14–15), then take the thread back through first bead. Couch between every bead to hold the circle in place, then take the needle through all of the gold beads, several times, to pull the beads into an even circle. Secure the thread.

3. With a board underneath for support, carefully shape the gilt passing around the petals into a pleasing outline, using a mellor or metal nailfile (being metal, the passing can be manipulated a little).

TO COMPLETE PEONY

Using nylon thread, stitch a 'wildberry' antique bead at the indentation between each petal around the outside edge of the peony (the hole in the bead parallel to the edge).

Border & Spangles

Five rows of assorted threads and wires are couched side by side to produce a narrow solid border. A beaded prunus blossom is worked at each corner.

Starting from the inside border line these rows comprise:

Row A: couched Japanese gold thread.

Row B: couched purple perle thread.

Row C: couched turquoise wrapped wire (this row is worked first).

Row D: couched burgundy wrapped pearl purl.

Row E: couched gilt twist.

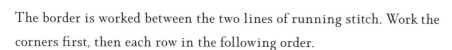

The border is worked between the two lines of running stitch. Work the corners first, then each row in the following order.

1. PRUNUS BLOSSOM CORNERS

Work as for the prunus blossom in the Persian Peony Tile with the following variations. For diagrams and more detailed instructions see pages 86–87.

- Using nylon thread, securely stitch a 2.5 mm gold bead in the centre of each of the four corners of the border.

- To form the blossom petals, stitch one wildberry seed bead next to the gold centre bead (the hole parallel to edge of gold bead). Bring the needle to the front, pass it through the wildberry bead then thread on seven more beads. Pass needle through the first bead again, forming a circle of beads. Take the needle through to the back and bring out on the other side of the circle of beads. Couch between each wildberry bead, then pass the needle through all eight beads several times to pull the beads into even circle. Secure the thread. Work a beaded blossom in each corner.

2. TURQUOISE WRAPPED WIRE (ROW C)

Wire, wrapped with turquoise thread, is couched along the centre of the border, between the beaded blossoms. All subsequent rows will be worked on either side of this row.

- Cut three 12 cm (4¾ in) lengths of wire. Holding the three wires together in a bundle, wrap the centre 3.7 cm (1½ in) with one strand of turquoise thread in a tapestry needle, temporarily securing each end of the thread with a half hitch (buttonhole loop). Try to keep the wires from twisting. Check the length of the wrapped section—it needs to fit between the beaded blossoms, along the centre of the border (unwrap thread if necessary).
- Carefully cut away one of the wires at each end of the wrapping (choose a wire that will be 'underneath' the wrapped section when it is applied), then bend the remaining tails of wire sharply at right angles to the wrapped section. Using a large yarn darner, insert the tails of wire (and wrapping thread tails) through to the back, close to the beaded blossom at each end—the wrapped section needs to be in the centre of the border. Bend the wires tails under the wrapped section—secure and trim. With one strand of turquoise thread, couch the wrapped wire in place, pulling the couching stitches firmly so that they blend into the wrapping. Check that the wrapped wire is straight.
- Work the remaining three sides of the border in the same way.

3. PURPLE PERLE THREAD (ROW B)

A row of purple perle thread is couched inside the row of turquoise wrapped wire.

- Using one strand of purple stranded thread in a crewel needle, couch a row of purple perle thread inside the turquoise row, working the couching stitches towards and slightly under the turquoise wrapped wire and 2–3 mm apart.
- Insert the tails of perle thread through to the back, close to the beaded blossoms, and secure.
- Work the remaining three sides of the border in the same way.

4. BURGUNDY WRAPPED PEARL PURL (ROW D)

A row of burgundy wrapped purl is couched outside the row of turquoise wrapped wire.

- Cut a 10 cm (4 in) length of gilt no. 3 pearl purl and stretch to 18 cm (7 in) by holding a coil of purl at each end and pulling apart gently. Cut the stretched purl into four lengths, each 3.7 cm (1½ in) long (one for each side of the border). Check that the extended length of purl will just fit between the beaded corners—trim or stretch if necessary.

- Using six strands of burgundy thread, each 20 cm (8 in) long, carefully wrap the extended purl between each coil, leaving a tail of thread at each end.
- With one strand of burgundy thread in a crewel needle, couch the wrapped purl on the outside of the turquoise row. To start, sink the tails of wrapping thread close to the beaded blossoms (hold at the back with masking tape) then work the couching stitches at an angle over the wrapped purl, one stitch every third or fourth coil. Secure the tails of wrapping thread.
- Work the remaining three sides of the border in the same way.

5. JAPANESE GOLD THREAD (ROW A)

- Using one strand of fine gold metallic thread in a size 9 sharps needle, couch a length of Japanese gold thread inside the row of purple perle, working the couching stitches towards the perle and 2–3 mm apart. Sink the tails of Japanese gold thread through to the back, close to the beaded blossoms and secure.
- Work the remaining three sides of the border in the same way.

6. GILT TWIST (ROW E)

- Using one strand of fine gold metallic thread in a sharps needle, couch a length of gilt twist outside the row of burgundy wrapped pearl purl, working the couching stitches towards the purl and at an angle across the twist, so that they sink into the coils of the twist. Sink the tails of gilt twist through to the back, close to the beaded blossoms and secure.
- Work the remaining three sides of the border in the same way.

Stitch gold spangles to the background, in each corner, with nylon or fine gold metallic thread, making three stitches into each spangle.

Carefully remove any silk running stitches if they show.

Knapweed Roundel

The knapweed blossoms decorating this small roundel have been embroidered in the colours found on an eighteenth century enamelled gold vessel from Mughal India. Embroidered on a satin background with silks, gold metallic threads, beads and tiny spangles, this design features the knapweed from the Persian Peony Tile, set within an elegant quatrefoil-shaped border. The roundel may be framed or mounted into the lid of a gilt bowl. It may also be used to decorate one side of a small mirror for an evening bag.

QUATREFOIL

The quatrefoil, an architectural term for a figure of four equal arcs or lobes, separated by cusps, is widely used in Islamic ornament.

QUATREFOIL

Pattern from a cotton-printer's block; Indian, nineteenth century.

KNAPWEED ROUNDEL SKELETON DIAGRAM
drawing actual size

Skeleton outline

KNAPWEED ROUNDEL
❧ REQUIREMENTS ❧

This is the complete list of requirements for this embroidery

+ ivory satin background fabric: 20 cm (8 in) square
+ quilter's muslin backing fabric: 20 cm (8 in) square
+ grey felt: 5 x 8 cm (2 x 3 in)
+ paper-backed fusible web: 5 x 8 cm (2 x 3 in)

+ 10 cm (4 in) or 12.5 cm (5 in) embroidery hoop
+ needles:
+ crewel/embroidery size 10

  sharps sizes 9 and 12

  sharp yarn darners sizes 14–18
+ beeswax
+ embroidery equipment

- ✛ aquamarine stranded thread (stems, leaves, knapweed): DMC 3812
- ✛ medium pink fine stranded thread (knapweed): Cifonda Art Silk 116
- ✛ dark purple stranded thread (border): DMC 791

- ✛ Japanese gold thread (T70 or No.8)
- ✛ gilt 3-ply twist
- ✛ gilt no.2 pearl purl
- ✛ fine gold metallic thread: YLI 601 Metallic Thread col. gold
- ✛ fine gold silk thread: YLI Silk Stitch 50 col. 79
- ✛ nylon clear thread: Madeira Monofil 60 col. 1001

- ✛ Mill Hill seed beads 00123 (cream)
- ✛ 2.5 mm medium pink beads
- ✛ 2 mm gold spangles

KNAPWEED ROUNDEL
❧ PREPARATION ❧

Mount the satin background fabric and the muslin backing into the embroidery hoop.

Trace the circle outline of the design onto tracing paper and transfer to the muslin backing. With fine silk thread, work a row of running stitches along the circle outline.

Using a fine lead pencil, trace the skeleton outline of the design (and the circle outline) onto tracing paper. Turn the tracing paper over and transfer the skeleton outline only to the background fabric with a stylus, lining up the traced circle outline with the stitched circle line (place a board underneath the hoop of fabric to provide a firm surface). Note: When marking the points for the knapweed blossoms, make a tiny pencil dot or insert a needle at each point and mark with a tacking stitch once the tracing paper has been removed.

Using gold silk thread in a small sharps needle, work a row of running stitches along the border line, working a back stitch into each corner of the quatrefoil to facilitate the working of the border. As the border threads will be applied over these running stitches, they need to be quite small and accurate.

Stems

Using one strand of aquamarine thread in a crewel needle, couch a double row of Japanese gold thread along the knapweed stem lines, working the centre stem first and making the stitches 2–3 mm apart. Begin by sinking the tails of gold thread through to the back at the lower edge of the knapweed flower, then couch along the stem line towards the base of the design, sinking the tails of gold thread as required. Secure all tails of thread to the backing fabric.

Leaves

With one strand of aquamarine thread, outline the leaves in split stitch then work a few padding stitches. Embroider each leaf in satin stitch, working the stitches at an angle across the leaf and enclosing the outline.

Knapweed

Work as for the knapweed in the Persian Peony Tile with the following variations. For diagrams and more detailed instructions see pages 84–86.

FLOWER BASE

1. Trace the knapweed base shapes onto paper-backed fusible web and fuse to grey felt. Cut out the shapes.

2. Using aquamarine thread, apply the felt shapes to the background (web side down) with a few stab stitches, then work a row of buttonhole stitch (stitches 1.5 mm apart) around the curved outside edge of the base (no stitches across the top V edge).

3. Cover the base in satin stitch, enclosing the buttonhole edge, and working 2–3 small stitches at each top peak.

4. With one strand of waxed fine gold metallic thread in a size 9 sharps needle, work straight stitches at an angle over the satin stitched base (lattice couching), securing the intersections with tiny stitches also worked in the gold thread.

Persian Carpet 16th~17th Cent?

PETALS

The knapweed petals are worked with evenly placed straight stitches, radiating out like 'spokes' from the V at the top edge of the base. A fine rayon thread (e.g. Cifonda) gives the best results. Use a size 10 needle when working these stitches as the thread tends to wear in a finer needle. Keep the stitches taut and change the thread regularly to prevent 'fluffy' stitches.

1. With one strand of fine medium pink thread, work a straight stitch from each dot to the top V edge (9 stitches), then work another stitch, the same length, between each of these stitches (8 stitches)—17 'spokes' in total.

2. Work another round of stitches between each 'spoke', 1–1.5 mm longer than the previous stitches.

3. Work 2 shorter stitches below the lower spoke on each side to complete the petals.

Border & Spangles

The centre of the border is worked over the line of running stitch—it is not necessary to remove these stitches.

1. Cut a 15 cm (6 in) length of gilt no. 2 pearl purl and stretch to 30 cm (12 in) by holding a coil of purl at each end and pulling apart gently. Using six strands of dark purple thread, carefully wrap the purl between each coil, leaving a tail of thread at each end (trim the final coil at each end to neaten, if necessary).

2. Using one strand of dark purple thread in a crewel needle, couch the wrapped purl along the stitched border line, carefully bending the corners of the quatrefoil with tweezers. To start, sink one tail of wrapping thread at one corner and hold at the back with masking tape. Work the couching stitches over the wrapped purl, one stitch every second or third coil, bringing the needle up and down on the line (2–3 mm apart) and working a couching stitch at each corner. Just before the starting point is reached again, unwrap the purple thread, cut the purl to the correct length, rewrap the purl and couch to the end of the line, sinking the tail of wrapping thread through to the back at the starting point. Secure both tails of purple thread.

3. Using waxed fine gold metallic thread, couch a 40 cm (16 in) length of gilt twist on the outside edge of the couched purl, starting at a corner and working the couching stitches towards the purl (the couching stitches may be worked diagonally, following the angle of the twist). Sink the tails of twist through to the back and secure.

4. Using nylon thread (or fine gold metallic thread), couch a 40 cm (16 in) length of Japanese gold thread on the inside edge of the couched purl, starting at another corner and working the couching stitches towards the purl. Sink the tails of gold thread through to the back and secure.

5. Stitch gold spangles to background with nylon or fine gold metallic thread, making three stitches into each spangle (secure the thread behind each spangle before moving on to the next one).

Prunus Blossom

Work as for the prunus blossom in the Persian Peony Tile with the following variations. For diagrams and more detailed instructions see pages 86–87. Work a beaded prunus blossom at each indentation of the quatrefoil.

1. Using nylon thread, stitch a 2.5 mm pink bead at each blossom centre point.

2. To form the blossom petals, stitch one cream seed bead next to the pink centre bead (with the hole parallel to edge of pink bead). Bring the needle to the front, pass it through the cream bead then thread on seven more cream beads. Pass needle through the first bead again, forming a circle of beads. Take the needle through to the back and bring out on the other side of the circle of beads. Couch between each cream bead, then pass the needle through all eight beads several times to pull the beads into even circle. Secure the thread. Repeat for the other three blossoms.

syrian

A recurring image in Islamic design is the pomegranate
enclosed in a pattern of radiating leaves (palmette motif). The
serrated leaves surrounding the pomegranate often resembled the
acanthus in shape. This section features the Syrian Pomegranate Tile, an
ornate panel inspired by a 17th century Syrian enamelled wall-tile.
Three smaller projects follow—Pomegranate Medallion, Iris Tile or
Book Cover and Cherry Flower Roundel—each designed around
a single motif from the Syrian Pomegranate Tile.

Syrian Pomegranate Tile

This ornate circular panel was inspired by a

seventeenth century Syrian enamelled wall-tile. Combining

stumpwork, goldwork and surface embroidery techniques, this tile is

worked on an ivory silk background with silks, gold metallic threads,

beads and tiny spangles. The design features a stylised pomegranate

flower, purple iris, white pear flowers with detached petals

and beaded prunus blossoms, and is enclosed by an ornate border

worked in gold metallic threads and beads.

TEXTILE WITH POMEGRANATE PALMETTE MOTIF
Persian, sixteenth century

This image, featuring a pomegranate palmette motif, was the inspiration for the
Syrian Pomegranate Tile design. By the early sixteenth century, silk textiles in a variety of
weights and weaves, and often containing gold- and silver-wrapped threads, were being woven in
north-west Turkey at Bursa, the western terminus of the raw silk trade route from the
East which supplied both the Ottoman and European markets. The sultans
distributed vast quantities of these woven silks as robes of honour.

Palmette: of Assyrian origin, this motif has many variations: basically,
it consists of an uneven number of narrow leaves springing from a tongue-like shape,
the whole device resembling a palm leaf or the palm of the hand outspread: the central leaf
is the largest, those on each side diminishing in size towards the outer edge.
In Persia, palmate ornament was often in the form of a series of lotus-like flowers.
D. Ware & M. Stafford, An Illustrated Dictionary of Ornament, page 161

SYRIAN POMEGRANATE TILE DIAGRAMS

drawings actual size

Skeleton outline

Pomegranate upper
petals padding

Pomegranate padding

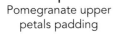

Pomegranate
leather shape

Detached iris petals

Detached pear
flower petal

Upper detached
pomegranate petals

Lower detached
pomegranate petals

SYRIAN POMEGRANATE TILE
❧ REQUIREMENTS ❧

This is the complete list of requirements for this embroidery

✛ ivory silk background fabric: 28 cm (11 in) square

✛ quilter's muslin (or calico) backing fabric: 28 cm (11 in) square

✛ quilter's muslin: four 20 cm (8 in) squares

✛ red felt: 10 x 8 cm (4 x 3 in)

✛ paper-backed fusible web: 10 x 8 cm (4 x 3 in)

✛ gold kid/leather: 2.5 cm (1 in) square

✛ 20 cm (8 in) embroidery hoop or stretcher bars

✛ 10 cm (4 in) embroidery hoops

✛ needles:

✛ crewel/embroidery size 10

sharps size 9 and 12

beading size 13

tapestry size 28

sharp yarn darners sizes 14–18

✛ beeswax

✛ embroidery equipment

✛ green stranded thread (stems, leaves, iris): Soie d'Alger 1826 or DMC 500

✛ medium orange stranded thread (pomegranate): Soie d'Alger 635 or DMC 946

✛ dark orange stranded thread (pomegranate, border): Soie d'Alger 636 or DMC 900

✛ russet stranded thread (pomegranate): Soie d'Alger 2636 or DMC 919

✛ dark purple stranded thread (iris): Soie d'Alger 1326 (no match in DMC)

✛ medium purple stranded thread (iris): Soie d'Alger 1325 (no match in DMC)

✛ cream stranded thread (pear flower): Soie d'Alger Crème/4102 or DMC 712

For ease of use, the requirements of each individual element are repeated under its heading—for example, Stems and Leaves requirements, Pomegranate requirements.

- ✣ Japanese gold T70
- ✣ gilt 3-ply twist
- ✣ gold couching thread 371
- ✣ gilt super pearl purl
- ✣ gilt no. 3 pearl purl
- ✣ fine gold metallic thread: YLI 601 Metallic Thread col. gold
- ✣ fine gold silk thread: YLI Silk Stitch 50 col. 79
- ✣ nylon clear thread: Madeira Monofil 60 col. 1001
- ✣ red sewing thread: Gutermann Polyester col. 365

- ✣ Mill Hill antique beads 03038 (ginger)
- ✣ Mill Hill petite beads 42028 (ginger)
- ✣ Mill Hill petite beads 40374 (purple/green)
- ✣ 3 mm gold beads
- ✣ 2.5 mm gold beads
- ✣ 2 mm gold beads
- ✣ 1.5 mm gold beads

- ✣ 6 mm gold cup sequins
- ✣ 5 mm purple/green cup sequins
- ✣ 2 mm gold

- ✣ 33 gauge white covered wire (iris): six 9 cm (3½ in) lengths
  (colour purple if desired, Copic V09 Violet)
- ✣ 33 gauge white covered wire (pomegranate): four 9 cm (3½ in) lengths
  (colour russet if desired, Copic E07 Light Mahogany)
- ✣ 33 gauge white covered wire (pear flowers). twenty 9 cm (3½ in) lengths

SYRIAN POMEGRANATE TILE
❦ PREPARATION ❦

Mount the silk background fabric and the muslin backing into the
20 cm (8 in) embroidery hoop or frame.

Trace the skeleton outline on to the background fabric,
taking care to align the design with the grain of the fabric (see Part 5:
Techniques, Equipment and Stitch Glossary).

Using gold silk thread in a small sharps needle, work a row of running stitches
along both border lines, working a back stitch into each corner of the scallops
to facilitate the working of the border. As the border threads will be applied
over these running stitches, they need to be quite small and accurate.

Stems & Leaves

REQUIREMENTS

✢ Japanese gold T70

✢ gilt 3-ply twist

✢ Green stranded thread: Soie d'Alger 1826 or DMC 500

STEMS

Using one strand of green thread, couch a double row of gold thread along all stem lines (except the prunus blossom stems, which have a single row), working the stitches 2–3 mm apart. Following the recommended order of work, begin by sinking the tails of gold thread through to the back at the lower edge of the specified flower, then couch along the stem line towards the base of the design, sinking the tails of gold thread as required. Trim and secure all tails of thread to the backing fabric.

ORDER OF WORK

1. Couch the pomegranate flower stem (a) with a double row of gilt 3-ply twist.

2. Couch the centre iris stem (b) with a double row of Japanese gold thread. All remaining stems are worked with Japanese gold thread.

3. Couch the upper pear flower stems (c, below the small circle) and the side iris stems (d), sinking the inner thread tails where these stems merge. Couch the remaining threads along the stem line until the pomegranate stem is reached, then sink both tails of thread.

4. Couch the lower pear flower stems (e, below the small circle) with a double row of gold thread until the pomegranate flower stem is reached. Sink the inner tail of thread then couch the remaining single row next to the pomegranate stem, sinking the tail of thread 2 mm (1/16 in) above the base of the pomegranate flower stem to form a neat end.

5. Using one strand of dark green thread in a crewel needle, work the pear flower leaf stems (above the small circles) in split stitch.

6. Work the prunus blossom stems after the blossoms are applied.

LEAVES

With one strand of dark green thread in a Crewel needle, outline all the leaves in split stitch then work a few padding stitches. Embroider each leaf in satin stitch, working the stitches at an angle across the leaf and enclosing the outline.

FLORAL-WORK FROM AN ENAMELLED TILE; SYRIAN, SEVENTEENTH CENTURY.

A recurring image in Islamic design is the stylised pomegranate or lotus shape enclosed in a pattern of radiating leaves —a variation of the palmette motif.

Pomegranate Flower

The pomegranate flower is worked in layers—lower background petals, upper background petals and base, padded pomegranate and detached petals.

REQUIREMENTS

- ✛ quilter's muslin (or calico) backing fabric: 28 cm (11 in) square
- ✛ red felt: 10 x 8 cm (4 x 3 in)
- ✛ paper-backed fusible web: 10 x 8 cm (4 x 3 in)
- ✛ medium orange stranded thread (pomegranate):
  Soie d'Alger 635 or DMC 946
- ✛ dark orange stranded thread (pomegranate, border):
  Soie d'Alger 636 or DMC 900
- ✛ russet stranded thread (pomegranate):
  Soie d'Alger 2636 or DMC 919
- ✛ gilt super pearl purl
- ✛ nylon clear thread: Madeira Monofil 60 col. 1001
- ✛ red sewing thread: Gutermann Polyester col. 365
- ✛ gold kid/leather—2.5 cm (1 in) square
- ✛ 3 mm gold beads
- ✛ 2 mm gold beads
- ✛ 6 mm gold cup sequins
- ✛ 5 mm purple/green cup sequin
- ✛ 33 gauge white covered wire (pomegranate): four 9 cm (3½ in) lengths
  (colour russet if desired, Copic E07 Light Mahogany)

LOWER BACKGROUND PETALS

Using medium orange thread in a crewel needle, outline the lower background petals in split back stitch (do not stitch around the base of the flower). Embroider each petal in padded satin stitch, working the stitches towards the centre line ----- and enclosing the outline.

base

UPPER BACKGROUND PETALS & POMEGRANATE

1. Trace shape A, shape B and shape C on to paper-backed fusible web and fuse to red felt. Cut out the shapes, taking care not to snip too far into the felt at the petal indentations as these need to be stitched.

2. Apply shape A (upper background petals and base padding), web side down, over the embroidered background petals, lining up the base of the padding with the base outline on the background. Stitch the padding in place with small, close (1–1.5 mm apart) stab stitches, using red sewing thread in a small sharps needle.

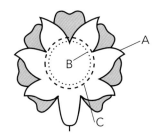

3. Apply the pomegranate padding (shapes B and C), web side down, over the petal padding, using the diagram as a guide to placement. Using red sewing thread and small, close stab stitches, apply the smaller circle of felt (B) first, then the larger shape (C) on top.

4. Trace shape D on to paper (or a Post-it note) and cut out on the line. Use this shape as a template to cut a pomegranate shape from gold leather (trim if necessary; it should be just large enough to fit over the padding). Using nylon thread in a small sharps needle, stab stitch the gold leather over the felt padding, easing the edge of the leather in close to the edge of the padding with a nailfile or mellor.

5. Each upper background petal edge is outlined with gilt super pearl purl, couched in place with waxed gold silk thread. Working the petals in the order as numbered (petals 1, 2 then 3), couch the purl along the top edge of the petal first then work the lower edge, using tweezers to form the point at the tip of the petal. All the ends of the purl touch the gold leather shape except the lower end of petal 2, which touches the edge of petal 1.

6. Using one strand of dark orange thread in a crewel needle, embroider each upper background petal, inside the purl outline, in satin stitch. Work the stitches from the edge of the gold leather towards the purl. Use a nailfile or mellor to neaten the edge of the gold leather (push in towards the padding) and to shape the purl around the petals.

FLOWER BASE

Using one strand of russet thread, work a row of buttonhole stitch around the base padding (just into the edge of the felt), making the stitches 1.5 mm apart. Embroider the base in satin stitch (enclosing the buttonhole stitch outline), first working horizontal padding stitches, then vertical satin stitches, worked towards the stem.

DETACHED PETALS

1. Mount a small square of muslin into a 10 cm (4 in) hoop and trace four detached petal shapes—a right and left upper petal and a right and a left lower petal.

2. Using one strand of russet thread, couch wire (coloured if desired) around the petal outline, leaving two wire tails at the base that touch but do not cross. Buttonhole stitch the wire to the muslin, then work a row of split stitch inside the wire. Work a few padding stitches then embroider the petal in satin stitch. Cut out the petals and shape slightly.

TO COMPLETE THE POMEGRANATE FLOWER

1. Using nylon thread in a small sharps needle, stitch three 2 mm gold beads at the top of the leather shape. Bring the needle out at the edge of the leather in the middle of petal 3, thread on the three gold beads, then insert the needle at the edge of the leather in the middle of the other petal 3 (the stitch will be longer than the beads). Make another stitch through all three beads, adjust the position of the beads at the top of the pomegranate then couch between each bead.

2. Using a large yarn darner, insert the upper detached petals through two holes, 2 mm apart, at the base of the pomegranate. Bend the wires back underneath the petals and secure.

3. Lifting the detached petals slightly away from the surface of the pomegranate, arrange the sequins (just above the upper detached petals) in the pattern as shown—the purple/green sequin at the bottom, two gold

sequins in the next row (under the first one), then one gold sequin at the top (under the previous row). Stitch in place as invisibly as possible, using nylon thread in a size 12 needle (two stitches in each sequin), stitching through all layers to the back (a thimble helps!).

4. Insert the two lower detached petals through one hole, just below the two upper petals. Bend the wires back underneath and secure. Shape the petals as desired. Finally, stitch a 3 mm gold bead in the space between the two upper detached petals at the base of the pomegranate.

Iris

REQUIREMENTS

+ quilter's muslin: 20 cm (8 in) square
+ dark purple stranded thread: Soie d'Alger 1326 (no match in DMC)
+ medium purple stranded thread: Soie d'Alger 1325 (no match in DMC)
+ green stranded thread: Soie d'Alger 1826 or DMC 500
+ gold couching thread 371
+ gilt super pearl purl
+ fine gold metallic thread: YLI 601 Metallic Thread col. gold
+ nylon clear thread: Madeira Monofil 60 col. 1001
+ Mill Hill petite beads 40374 (purple/green)
+ 2 mm gold beads
+ 33 gauge white covered wire (iris): six 9 cm (3½ in) lengths (colour purple if desired, Copic V09 Violet)

BACKGROUND PETALS

1. Using one strand of medium purple thread in a crewel needle, outline the three background petals in back stitch. Embroider each petal in long and short stitch, enclosing the outline, commencing with medium purple thread at the outer edge of each petal, blending to dark purple at the centre.

SYRIAN WALL TILES, SIXTEENTH CENTURY.

The Syrian tile industry flourished in Damascus from the fourteenth century. The painted enamelled tiles often featured the arabesque and floral designs. The iris, with its readily stylised, symmetrical form, was a popular floral motif, often depicted in rich manganese purple.

2. Using nylon thread in a small sharps needle, couch a row of gold couching thread 371 around the edge of all three background petals, sinking the tails of thread at the lower corners.

3. Using nylon thread, stitch a purple/green petite bead in the centre of each petal, about 4 mm down from the top edge (make about four stitches to be firm). Stitch a loop of gold couching thread around this bead as follows:

- Cut a 10 cm (4 in) length of gold couching thread and thread both tails into the smallest yarn darner.
- Insert the darner 1 mm below the bead, leaving a loop of gold thread on the surface. Couch this loop of gold thread around the bead with nylon thread.

Secure the tails of gold thread at the back of the petal then trim.

DETACHED PETALS

1. Mount a small square of muslin into a 10 cm (4 in) hoop and trace a pair of detached lower petals for each iris. Using medium purple thread, couch wire (coloured if desired) around the petal outline, leaving two tails of wire that touch but do not cross. Buttonhole stitch the wire to the muslin, then work a row of split stitch inside the wire. Embroider the petal in long and short stitch, blending from dark purple, at the base of the petal, to medium purple towards the outer edge.

2. Stitch a petite bead, surrounded by a gold couching thread loop, in the centre of each detached petal (as for the background petals).

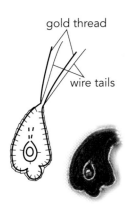

gold thread

wire tails

3. Using nylon thread in a small sharps needle, couch a row of gold couching thread around the edge of each petal, leaving two thread tails at the base. Work the couching stitches into the buttonhole edge, between the wire and the ridge of the buttonhole stitches, with firm, close stitches (1.5 mm apart). Carefully cut out the petals, taking care not to cut any of the thread or wire tails or the couching stitches.

BASE

The base of the iris is worked in raised stem stitch.

1. With one strand of green thread in a crewel needle, outline the edge of the base in back stitch.

2. With a double strand of green thread, work 6 stitches, inside the outline, to pad the base, working the stitches from the stem end towards the background petals. Leave a small gap between the edge of the padding and embroidered background petals to insert the detached petals.

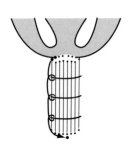

3. With one strand of green thread, work three evenly spaced couching stitches over the padding (and the outline). Changing to a tapestry needle, work a row of raised stem stitch over these couching stitches, starting near the background petals and working towards the stem. Work seven more rows of raised stem stitch to cover the base.

4. With one strand of waxed gold metallic thread in a size 9 sharps needle, work diagonal stitches over the base (lattice couching), working the stitches from the stem end towards the petals.

TO COMPLETE THE IRIS

1. Using a large yarn darner, apply the detached petals (through two separate holes), in the small gap between the top edge of the base and the background petals (insert both the wires and the gold thread tails through the same hole for each petal). Bend the wires and the tails of gold thread behind nearest background petal and secure (do not trim the wires until the end).

2. With dark purple thread in a small sharps needle, stitch a 2 mm gold bead between the detached petals (working the stitches vertically). Work 4 or 5 stitches, through the bead, to fill any gaps at the base of the background petals.

3. Using nylon thread in a small sharps needle, couch a loop of gilt super pearl purl around the gold bead as follows:

- Bring the needle out below the gold bead, thread on a 1 cm (⅜ in) length of purl and curve it into a loop (around a yarn darner), then insert the needle below the gold bead (position the exit and entry points of the needle to allow the cut ends of the purl loop to sit side by side).
- Couch the loop around the bead with a few stitches.

4. Shape the detached petals then trim the wire tails.

Pear Flowers

✣ requirements

✣ quilter's muslin: two 20 cm (8 in) squares

✣ cream stranded thread: Soie d'Alger Crème/4102 or DMC 712

✣ nylon clear thread: Madeira Monofil 60 col. 1001

✣ Mill Hill petite beads 42028 (ginger)

✣ 2 mm gold beads

✣ 33 gauge white covered wire (pear flowers): twenty 9 cm (3½ in) lengths

DETACHED PETALS

1. Mount a square of muslin into a 10 cm (4 in) hoop and trace ten pear flower petal outlines (twenty detached petals are required—work the remaining ten petals on the other square of muslin). As the petals are worked in cream thread, use the minimum amount of lead when tracing to prevent soiling the edges, and change the thread regularly.

2. Using one strand of cream thread in a crewel needle, couch wire around the petal outline, leaving two wire tails at the base that touch but do not cross. Check that the distance between the outside edges of the wires, across the petal, is about 6 mm (¼ in)—if larger, the petals will overlap (instead of being side by side) when they are applied. Overcast stitch the wire to the fabric then work a row of split stitch inside the wire.

3. Using a new length of thread, embroider the petals in padded satin stitch, working the stitches towards the base of the petal (make every alternate stitch slightly shorter so that they fan inside the shape). Cut out the petals.

FRUIT BLOSSOM ON PERSIAN CARPET; SIXTEENTH CENTURY.

Islamic craftsmen made great use of sprigs of fruit blossom in their designs, using the curved branches of almond, peach, pear and plum blossoms to embellish any empty spaces.

TO COMPLETE THE PEAR FLOWER

1. Using a large yarn darner, insert the tails of five petals through a circle of five individual holes (as close to each other as possible). Bend the wire tails back underneath each petal and secure (do not cut the wire tails until the centre is worked).

2. Using tweezers, shape the petals, pushing them gently towards the centre (they should be sitting side by side, not overlapping). Using nylon thread and a small sharps needle, sew a 2 mm gold bead into the centre of the flower. Stitch a ginger petite bead (42028) at the base of every petal, carefully bringing the needle out through the petal (from the back) and stitching towards the gold bead (make two stitches in each bead). After a final shaping of the petals, trim the wire tails (shorter than the span of the flower).

Prunus Blossom

Work all the beaded blossoms before working the prunus blossom stems.

REQUIREMENTS

+ Mill Hill antique beads 03038 (ginger)
+ 2.5 mm gold beads
+ 2 mm gold beads
+ 1.5 mm gold beads
+ nylon clear thread: Madeira Monofil 60 col. 1001
+ green stranded thread: Soie d'Alger 1826 or DMC 500
+ Japanese gold T70

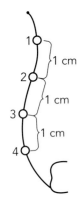

1. Apply all the gold centre beads first, stitching them in the positions as marked on the stem line. Using nylon thread in a small sharps needle, stitch a 2 mm gold bead for the centre of the upper blossom (1), and a 2.5 mm gold bead for the centres of the lower three blossoms (2, 3 and 4)—four stitches in each bead to make them secure. Check that the centre points of all the gold beads are 1 cm apart and that the centres on both stems are level with each other.

2. The petals are worked with ginger antique beads (03038) using nylon thread. To form the petals on blossom 4, stitch one ginger bead next to the gold centre bead (with the hole parallel to edge of the gold bead). Bring the needle to the front, pass it through the ginger bead then thread on seven more ginger beads. Pass needle through the first bead again, forming a circle of beads. Take the needle through to the back and bring out on the other side of the circle of beads. Couch between each ginger bead, then pass the needle through all eight beads several times to pull the beads into an even circle. Secure thread. Blossom 3 is worked the same way.

3. Following the same method, work blossoms 1 and 2, applying seven (not eight) beads for the petals.

4. The blossom stems are worked with a single row of Japanese gold thread, couched in place with one strand of green thread. To work the blossom

Prunus blossom from a painted earthenware tile. Turkish, 16th c.

stems, thread a length of Japanese gold thread into a small yarn darner (to reduce the risk of damaging the thread), then make a stitch between the edge of the lower pomegranate petal and the edge of blossom 4 (pull the gold thread through the fabric carefully). Work a stitch between each blossom, then a stitch from the edge of blossom 1 to the end of the stem, adjusting the tension of the gold thread as you go. Couch the gold thread in place with one strand of green thread. Secure the tails of gold thread at the back.

5. To form the prunus bud, stitch two ginger beads at the end of the stem, the base of the beads touching and the top edges slightly apart (like a V), using nylon thread. Using a beading needle, stitch a 1.5 mm gold bead above them to form the tip.

gold
ginger

Border & Spangles

The border is worked over the two lines of running stitch—it is not necessary to remove these stitches.

REQUIREMENTS

+ Japanese gold T70
+ gilt 3-ply twist
+ gilt no. 3 pearl purl
+ fine gold metallic thread: YLI 601 Metallic Thread col. gold
+ dark orange stranded thread: Soie d'Alger 636 or DMC 900
+ nylon clear thread: Madeira Monofil 60 col. 1001
+ 3 mm gold beads
+ 1.5 mm gold beads
+ 2 mm gold spangles

INNER BORDER LINE

Couch 45 cm (18 in) lengths of Japanese gold thread and gilt 3-ply twist together over the inner line (Japanese gold on the inside), using waxed, fine gold metallic thread in a size 9 sharps needle. Work the couching stitches 2–3 mm apart, over both threads except at the corners of the scallops, where each thread is first couched individually then a stitch is worked over both, to achieve a sharper point. Sink the tails of both gold threads after the couching is complete and secure.

OUTER BORDER LINE

1. Cut a 20 cm (8 in) length of gilt no. 3 pearl purl and stretch to 43 cm (17 in) by holding a coil of purl at each end and pulling apart gently. Using five strands of dark orange thread, 75–80 cm (30 in) long, carefully wrap the purl between each coil, leaving a 10 cm (4 in) tail of thread at each end (trim the final coil of purl at each end to neaten, if necessary).

2. Using one strand of dark orange thread in a crewel needle, couch the wrapped purl over the outer line, bending the purl into shape at the corners with tweezers. To start, sink one tail of wrapping thread at one scallop corner and hold at the back with masking tape. Work the couching stitches at an angle over the wrapped purl, one stitch every third or fourth coil, bringing the needle up and down on the line (2–3 mm apart) and working a couching stitch at each corner. Just before the starting corner is reached, unwrap the dark orange thread, cut the purl to the correct length, rewrap the purl and couch to the end of the line, sinking the tail of wrapping thread through to the back. Secure both tails of dark orange thread.

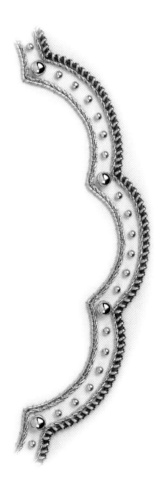

3. Using waxed, fine gold metallic thread in a size 9 sharps needle, couch a length of gilt 3-ply twist along the inside edge of the wrapped purl, working the couching stitches towards the purl. Sink the tails at a corner.

4. Using nylon thread in a small sharps needle, stitch a 3 mm gold bead at each scallop corner of the outer border. Make one long stitch through the bead from the corner of gilt twist into the opposite corner of the inner border, then work two or three shorter stitches to position the bead accurately.

5. Using nylon thread in a beading needle, stitch a row of six 1.5 mm gold beads inside the border lines between each large gold bead (the holes in the beads lie at right angles to the border). Fine needles can be used to mark the position of the small beads evenly between the large beads. Working all stitches towards the inner border, first stitch all the beads in place, with quite long stitches, in a clockwise direction (also going through each 3 mm bead again). Stitch back through all the beads again, in an anti-clockwise direction, making the stitches shorter to accurately position the beads (the threads will cross at the back, making the beads sit very evenly).

6. Stitch gold spangles to background with nylon or fine gold metallic thread, making three stitches into each spangle (secure the thread behind each spangle before moving on to the next one).

Pomegranate Medallion

This small ornate medallion features a slightly enlarged version
of the pomegranate from the Syrian Pomegranate Tile, worked in soft
sage green and manganese purple—colours which first appeared in
Islamic ceramics in the 1540s. Combining stumpwork, goldwork
and surface embroidery techniques, this circular panel is worked on
an ivory silk background with silks, gold metallic threads and beads.
The design comprises a stylised pomegranate flower with
detached petals, surrounded by a border of beaded prunus
blossoms. The finished piece may be framed or inserted
into the base of a glass paperweight.

CHRISTOPHER DRESSER:
FOUR STUDIES IN THE MANNER OF PERSIAN
CERAMIC DECORATION
Modern Ornamentation, 1886.

POMEGRANATE MEDALLION DIAGRAMS
drawings actual size

Skeleton outline

Pomegranate upper
petals padding

B

Pomegranate padding

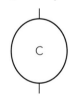

C

D

Pomegranate
leather shape

Upper detached
pomegranate petals

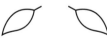

Lower detached
pomegranate petals

POMEGRANATE MEDALLION
❧ REQUIREMENTS ❧

This is the complete list of requirements for this embroidery

- ✛ ivory silk background fabric: 20 cm (8 in) square
- ✛ quilter's muslin (or calico) backing fabric: 20 cm (8 in) square
- ✛ quilter's muslin: 20 cm (8 in) square
- ✛ grey felt: 10 x 8 cm (4 x 3 in)
- ✛ paper-backed fusible web: 10 x 8 cm (4 x 3 in)

- ✛ gold kid/leather: 2.5 cm (1 in) square
- ✛ 13 cm (5 in) embroidery hoop
- ✛ 10 cm (4 in) embroidery hoop
- ✛ needles:
  crewel/embroidery size 10
  sharps size 12
  beading size 13
  sharp yarn darners sizes 14–18
- ✛ beeswax
- ✛ embroidery equipment

- ✛ green stranded thread (pomegranate, stems, leaves):
  Soie d'Alger 516 or DMC 469
- ✛ medium mauve stranded thread (pomegranate):
  Soie d'Alger 5114 or DMC 3041
- ✛ dark mauve stranded thread (pomegranate):
  Soie d'Alger 5115 or DMC 3740 (closest colour)

- ✛ Japanese gold T70
- ✛ gilt super pearl purl
- ✛ fine gold silk thread: YLI Silk Stitch 50 col. 79
- ✛ Nylon clear thread: Madeira Monofil 60 col. 1001
- ✛ Grey sewing thread: Gutermann Polyester col. 127

- ✛ Mill Hill antique beads 03038 (ginger)
- ✛ Mill Hill petite beads 40374 (purple/green)
- ✛ 4 mm bronze bead
- ✛ 2.5 mm gold beads
- ✛ 2 mm gold beads
- ✛ 1.5 mm gold beads
- ✛ 6 mm transparent bronze cup sequins
- ✛ 5 mm purple/green cup sequin

- ✛ 33 gauge white covered wire (pomegranate):
  four 9 cm (3½ in) lengths (colour mauve if desired, Copic V09 Violet)

POMEGRANATE MEDALLION
❧ PREPARATION ❧

Mount the silk background fabric and the muslin backing into the 13 cm (5 in) embroidery hoop.

Trace the circle outline of the design onto tracing paper and transfer to the muslin backing. With fine silk thread, work a row of running stitches along the circle outline.

Using a fine lead pencil, trace the skeleton outline of the design (and the circle outline) onto tracing paper. Turn the tracing paper over and transfer the skeleton outline only to the background fabric with a stylus, lining up the traced circle outline with the stitched circle line (place a board underneath the frame of fabric to provide a firm surface).

Note: When marking the points for the line of petite beads between the pomegranate and the beaded blossoms, make a very small pencil dot or insert a needle at each point and mark on the backing fabric.

Pomegranate Flower

Work as for the pomegranate flower in the Syrian Pomegranate Tile with the following variations. For diagrams and more detailed instructions see pages 135–138.

LOWER BACKGROUND PETALS

Using green thread, outline the lower background petals in split back stitch (do not stitch around the base of the flower). Embroider each petal in padded satin stitch, working the stitches towards the centre line ----- and enclosing the outline.

UPPER BACKGROUND PETALS AND POMEGRANATE

1. Trace shape A, shape B and shape C on to paper-backed fusible web and fuse to grey felt. Cut out the shapes, taking care not to snip too far into the felt at the petal indentations as these need to be stitched.

2. Apply shape A (upper background petals and base padding), web side down, over the embroidered background petals, lining up the base of the padding with the base outline on the background.
Stitch the padding in place with small, close (1–1.5 mm apart) stab stitches, using grey sewing thread.

3. Apply the pomegranate padding (B and C), web side down, over the petal padding, referring to the diagram for placement. Using grey sewing thread and small, close stab stitches, apply the smaller circle of felt (B) first, then the larger shape (C) on top.

4. Trace shape D on to paper (or a Post-it note) and cut out on the line. Use this shape as a template to cut a pomegranate shape from gold leather (trim if necessary; it should be just large enough to fit over the padding).
Using nylon thread, stab stitch the gold leather over the felt padding, easing the edge of the leather in close to the edge of the padding with a nailfile or mellor.

5. Each upper background petal edge is outlined with gilt super pearl purl,

Pomegranate from an enamelled tile; Turkish, sixteenth century.

couched in place with waxed gold silk thread. Working the petals in the order as numbered (1, 2 then 3), couch the purl along the top edge of the petal first then work the lower edge, using tweezers to form the point at the tip of the petal. All the ends of the purl touch the gold leather shape except the lower end of petal 2, which touches the edge of petal 1.

6. Using one strand of medium mauve thread, embroider each upper background petal, inside the purl outline, in satin stitch. Work the stitches from the edge of the gold leather towards the purl. Use a nailfile or mellor to neaten the edge of the gold leather (push in towards the padding) and to shape the purl around the petals.

FLOWER BASE

Using one strand of dark mauve thread, work a row of buttonhole stitch around the base padding (just into the edge of the felt), making the stitches 1.5 mm apart. Embroider the base in satin stitch (enclosing the buttonhole stitch outline), first working horizontal padding stitches, then vertical satin stitches, worked towards the stem.

DETACHED PETALS

1. Mount a small square of muslin into a 10 cm (4 in) hoop and trace four detached petal shapes—a right and left upper petal and a right and a left lower petal.

2. Using one strand of dark mauve thread, couch wire around the petal outline, leaving two wire tails at the base that touch but do not cross. Buttonhole stitch the wire to the muslin, then work a row of split stitch inside the wire. Work a few padding stitches, then embroider the petal in satin stitch. Cut out the petals and shape slightly.

TO COMPLETE THE POMEGRANATE FLOWER

1. Using nylon thread in a small sharps needle, stitch three 2 mm gold beads at the top of the leather shape. Bring the needle out at the edge of the leather in the middle of petal 3, thread on the three gold beads, then insert the needle at the edge of the leather in the middle of the other petal 3 (the stitch will be longer than the beads). Make another stitch through all three beads, adjust the position of the beads at the top of the pomegranate then couch between each bead.

2. Using a large yarn darner, insert the upper detached petals through two holes, 2 mm apart, at the base of the pomegranate. Bend the wires back underneath the petals and secure.

3. Lifting the detached petals slightly away from the surface of the pomegranate, arrange the sequins (just above the upper detached petals) in the pattern as shown—the purple/green sequin at the bottom, two transparent bronze sequins in the next row (under the first one), then one transparent bronze sequin at the top (under the previous row). Stitch in place as invisibly as possible, using nylon thread in a size 12 needle (two stitches in each sequin), stitching through all layers to the back (a thimble helps!).

4. Insert the two lower detached petals through one hole, just below the two upper petals. Bend the wires back underneath and secure. Shape the petals as desired. Finally, stitch a 3 or 4 mm bronze bead in the space between the two upper detached petals at the base of the pomegranate.

Leaves & Beads

1. With one strand of green thread in a crewel needle, outline the leaves at the base of the pomegranate in split stitch then work a few padding stitches. Embroider each leaf in satin stitch, working the stitches at an angle across the leaf and enclosing the outline.

2. With one strand of nylon thread in a sharps needle, stitch a row of purple/green petite beads on either side of the pomegranate—above the tips of the leaves. Apply each bead with two stitches, with the hole in the bead at right angles to the row.

Stem

Stitch the pomegranate stem after the lower beaded prunus blossom has been worked.

Cut a 10 cm (4 in) length of Japanese gold thread and fold in half. Using one strand of green thread, work a couching stitch over the fold to attach the gold thread to the base of the stem line (next to the beaded blossom). Couch the double row of gold thread along the stem line, working the stitches 2–3 mm apart, sinking the tails of thread through to the back at the lower edge of the pomegranate base. Trim and secure the tails to the backing fabric.

Prunus Blossom

Work as for the prunus blossom in the Syrian Pomegranate Tile with the following variations. For diagrams and more detailed instructions see pages 144–145.

Note: Work all the beaded blossoms before working the prunus blossom stems.

1. Apply all the gold centre beads first, stitching them in the positions as marked on the stem line—2.5 mm gold beads for the centres of blossoms 1, 2 and 3, and 2 mm gold beads for the centres of blossoms 4 and 5. Check that the centre points of all the gold beads are 1.5 cm apart and that the centres on both stems are level with each other.

2. The petals are worked with ginger antique beads (03038)

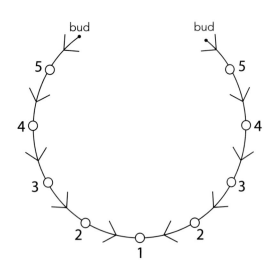

using nylon thread. To form the petals on blossom 1, stitch one ginger bead next to the gold centre bead (with the hole parallel to edge of the gold bead). Bring the needle to the front, pass it through the ginger bead then thread on seven more ginger beads. Pass needle through the first bead again, forming a circle of beads. Take the needle through to the back and bring out on the other side of the circle of beads. Couch between each ginger bead, then pass the needle through all eight beads several times to pull the beads into an even circle. Secure thread. Blossoms 2 are worked the same way.

3. Following the same method, work blossoms 3, 4 and 5, applying seven (not eight) beads for the petals.

4. Using one strand of green thread, couch a single row of Japanese gold thread between each beaded blossom to form the stem, taking the gold thread through to the back at the edges of the blossoms. Thread the Japanese gold thread into a small yarn darner (to reduce the risk of damaging the thread), then make a stitch between each blossom, starting at the edge of the lower blossom 1 and pulling the gold thread through the fabric carefully (adjust the tension of the gold thread as it is couched in place). To complete the stem, make a stitch from the edge of blossom 5 to the end of the stem line. Repeat for the other side. Secure the tails of gold thread at the back.

5. To form the prunus bud, stitch two ginger beads at the each end of the stem, the base of the beads touching and the top edges slightly apart (like a V), using nylon thread. Stitch a 1.5 mm gold bead above them to form the tip.

6. Using one strand of green thread, embroider the leaves on either side of the stem in satin stitch. Work each leaf with about 9 satin stitches, using the line as a guide, and making the final two satin stitches slightly longer to form a sharp point.

Iris Tile or Book Cover

This elegant tile features a slightly enlarged version of the iris

from the Syrian Pomegranate Tile. Combining goldwork and surface

embroidery techniques, this rectangular panel is worked on a dark

cream silk background with silks, gold metallic threads and beads.

The design comprises a stylised iris flower and buds, enclosed

by an ogival border worked in beads, gimp and gold metallic threads.

As I wished to use this panel as a book cover, the lower

petals of the iris have been embroidered on the silk background

rather than being detached. The finished piece may also be

framed or used as the front of a small evening bag.

IRIS TILE *or* BOOK COVER DIAGRAM
drawing actual size

Skeleton outline

Detached lower iris
petal outline

IRIS BOOK COVER MEASUREMENTS DIAGRAM
enlarge drawing 120%

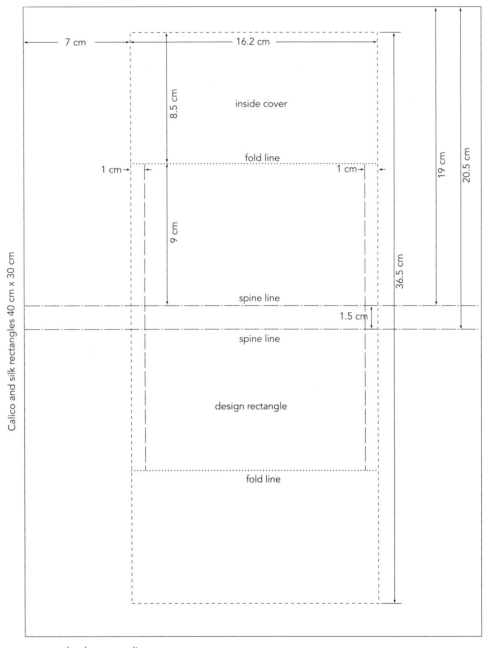

7 cm

16.2 cm

8.5 cm

inside cover

19 cm

20.5 cm

fold line

1 cm

1 cm

9 cm

36.5 cm

spine line

1.5 cm

spine line

Calico and silk rectangles 40 cm x 30 cm

design rectangle

fold line

- - - - - book cover outline
——— stitching line

IRIS TILE *or* BOOK COVER
❦ REQUIREMENTS ❦

This is the complete list of requirements for this embroidery

✢ dark cream silk background fabric: 30 cm (12 in) square for tile panel or 30 x 40 cm (12 x 15¾ in) for book cover

✢ plain calico backing fabric: 30 cm (12 in) square for panel or 30 x 40 cm (12 x 15¾ in) for book cover

- -

✢ 23 cm (9 in) or 25 cm (10 in) embroidery hoop

✢ needles:
crewel/embroidery size 10
sharps sizes 9 and 12
tapestry size 28
sharp yarn darners sizes 14–18

✢ beeswax

✢ embroidery equipment

- -

✢ olive green stranded thread (stems, leaves, iris):
Soie d'Alger 2214 or DMC 730

✢ medium burgundy stranded thread (iris): Soie d'Alger 4645 or DMC 3802

✢ dark burgundy stranded thread (iris): Soie d'Alger 4646 or DMC 902

- -

✢ variegated plum-caramel viscose gimp (border): Stef Francis Viscose Gimp col. 01 or substitute DMC Perle 3 col. 223 or 407

✢ caramel rayon machine thread (border): Madeira Rayon No.40 col. 1126

✢ Japanese gold T70

❧ OPTIONS ❧

If you wish to make a book cover, the panel has been designed to fit
a 9 cm x 14 cm (3½ x 5½ in) Moleskine® diary or address book.
You will also need dark cream sewing thread.

If the panel is to be framed, you may choose to work detached lower petals,
following the instructions for the iris in the Syrian Pomegranate Tile
(see page 138). Use the detached petal outline on page 162 and two
10 cm (4 in) lengths of 33 gauge covered wire. Remember to
omit the lower petal outlines from the skeleton outline.

+ gold couching thread 371
+ gilt super pearl purl
+ gilt no. 3 pearl purl
+ fine gold metallic thread: YLI 601 Metallic Thread col. gold
+ fine gold silk thread: YLI Silk Stitch 50 col. 79
+ nylon clear thread: Madeira Monofil 60 col. 1001
+
+ Mill Hill antique beads 3036 (variegated burgundy)
+ Mill Hill petite beads 40374 (purple/burgundy)
+ 2.5 mm gold beads

IRIS TILE
❧ PREPARATION ❧

Mount the silk background fabric and the calico backing into the embroidery hoop.

Cut a template from thin card, 9 x 14.3 cm (3½ x 5 ⅝ in). Place the template on the calico backing fabric (checking that it is aligned with the straight grain of the silk fabric at the front) and draw around the rectangle with a fine lead pencil. Using gold silk thread in a small sharps needle, work a row of small running stitches along the pencil lines, to form a stitched rectangle on the front fabric. This will be used as a reference grid when transferring the skeleton outline of the design.

IRIS BOOK COVER
❧ PREPARATION ❧

Place the calico rectangle on top of the silk rectangle and secure to
a table top with pieces of masking tape (the short ends of the rectangle
forming the side edges). With a fine lead pencil and ruler, draw the book
cover outlines, stitching lines and fold lines onto the calico as follows:

• Draw two vertical lines in the centre of the calico, one line 19 cm (7½ in)
away from the right side of the rectangle and the other line 20.5 cm (8 in)
away. These parallel lines,(1.5 cm apart) form the spine of the book cover.
Using these spine lines as a guide, draw the fold lines and the side
outlines using the measurements shown on the diagram.

• Draw a line 7 cm (2¾ in) down from the top edge of the calico
—this will be the top outline. Using the top outline as a guide,
draw in the lower outline and both stitching lines.

Using silk tacking thread in a small sharps needle, work a row of small
running stitches along the spine lines, fold lines and stitching lines
(stitching through the calico and silk). Note that the design panel is the
rectangle (9 cm x 14.2 cm (3½ x 5 ⅝ in) to the left of the left spine line.

Mount the silk and calico 'sandwich' into the embroidery hoop,
silk side uppermost, with the design panel in the centre of the hoop.
Check that the design panel 'rectangle' has not been
distorted and is the right way up.

❧ TO TRANSFER ❧ THE DESIGN

Using a fine lead pencil, trace the skeleton outline (including the dots for the beads) and rectangle outline onto tracing paper. Turn the tracing paper over and transfer the skeleton outline only to the background fabric with a stylus, lining up the traced rectangle with the stitched rectangle (place a board underneath the frame of fabric to provide a firm surface).

Note: When marking the dots for the row of petite beads, make a very small pencil dot or insert a needle at each point and mark the dots on the backing fabric.

Using gold silk thread, work a row of running stitches along the border line surrounding the iris. As the border will be worked over these running stitches, they need to be quite small and accurate.

Stems

Using one strand of olive green thread in a crewel needle, couch a double row of Japanese gold thread along the iris stem lines, working the centre stem first and making the stitches 2–3 mm apart. Begin by sinking the tails of gold thread through to the back at the lower edge of the iris flower or bud, then couch along the stem line towards the base of the design, sinking the tails of gold thread as required. Secure all tails of thread to the backing fabric.

Leaves

With one strand of olive green thread, outline the leaves in split stitch then work a few padding stitches. Embroider each leaf in satin stitch, working the stitches at an angle across the leaf, enclosing the outline.

Iris Flower

FLOWER PETALS

1. Using one strand of medium burgundy thread in a crewel needle, outline the five background petals in back stitch. Embroider each petal in long and short stitch (enclosing the outline), commencing with medium burgundy thread at the outer edge of each petal, blending to dark burgundy at the centre.

2. Using nylon thread in a small sharps needle, couch a row of gold couching thread 371 around the edge of both lower petals, sinking the tails of thread at the inner corners. Couch a row of thread around the three upper petals, sinking the tails of thread next to the edge of the lower petals.

3. Using nylon thread, stitch a purple/burgundy petite bead in the centre of each petal, about 4 mm down from the outer edge (make about four stitches to be firm). Stitch a loop of gold couching thread around this bead as follows:

Iris on Persian tile, sixteenth century.

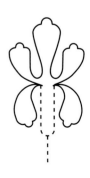

- Cut a 10 cm (4 in) length of gold couching thread and thread both tails into the smallest yarn darner.
- Insert the darner 1 mm below the bead, leaving a loop of gold thread on the surface. Couch this loop of gold thread around the bead with nylon thread. Secure the tails of gold thread at the back of the petal then trim.

FLOWER BASE

The base of the iris flower is worked in raised stem stitch.

1. With one strand of olive green thread, outline the edge of the flower base in back stitch.

2. With a double strand of olive green thread, work six stitches, inside the outline, to pad the flower base.

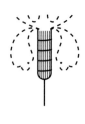

3. With one strand of olive green thread, work four evenly spaced couching stitches over the padding (and the outline). Changing to a tapestry needle, work a row of raised stem stitch over these couching stitches, starting next to the background petals and working towards the stem. Work eight more rows of raised stem stitch to cover the flower base.

4. With one strand of waxed gold metallic thread in a size 9 sharps needle, work diagonal stitches over the flower base (lattice couching), working the stitches from the stem end towards the petals.

TO COMPLETE THE IRIS FLOWER

1. With nylon thread in a small sharps needle, stitch a 2.5 mm gold bead between the detached petals (working the stitches vertically).

2. Using nylon thread, couch a loop of Gilt Super Pearl Purl around the gold bead as follows:
- Bring the needle out below the gold bead, thread on a 1.3 cm (½ in) length of purl, curve it into a loop (around a yarn darner), then insert the needle below the gold bead (position the exit and entry points of the needle to allow the cut ends of the purl loop to sit side by side).
- Couch the loop around the bead with a few stitches.

Iris Bud

The top of each bud is worked in satin stitch; the base is worked in raised stem stitch.

1. With one strand of olive green thread, outline the edge of the bud base (including the centre V) in back stitch.

2. With one strand of dark burgundy thread, work the top of the bud in satin stitch—ten satin stitches worked from the V of the base towards the tip of the bud.

3. With a double strand of olive green thread, work six stitches, inside the outline, to pad the bud base.

4. With one strand of olive green thread, work three evenly spaced couching stitches over the padding (and the outline). Changing to a tapestry needle, work a row of raised stem stitch over these couching stitches, starting next to the bud petals and working towards the stem. Work seven more rows of raised stem stitch to cover the bud base.

5. With one strand of waxed gold metallic thread in a size 9 sharps needle, work diagonal stitches over the base (lattice couching), working the stitches from the stem end towards the petals.

Border

Five rows of various threads and beads are stitched side by side, to form a narrow, solid band between the beaded prunus blossoms at the top and bottom points of the ogival border. The border is worked using the outline of running stitch as a guide. Work the beaded blossoms first first, then each row in the following order.

1. PRUNUS BLOSSOMS

Work as for the prunus blossom in the Syrian Pomegranate Tile with the following variations. For diagrams and more detailed instructions see pages 144–145.

- Using nylon thread, stitch 2.5 mm gold beads at the upper and lower points of the stitched border outline for the centres of the blossoms.

- To form the petals, stitch one burgundy antique bead next to the gold centre bead (with the hole parallel to edge of the gold bead). Bring the needle to the front, pass it through the burgundy bead then thread on seven more burgundy beads. Pass needle through the first bead again, forming a circle of beads. Take the needle through to the back and bring out on the other side of the circle of beads. Couch between each burgundy bead, then pass the needle through all eight beads several times to pull the beads into an even circle. Secure thread. Repeat for the other blossom.

2. STITCHED ANTIQUE BEADS

A row of variegated burgundy antique beads (3036) is stitched over the line of running stitch, between the beaded blossoms. All subsequent rows will be worked on either side of this row to form the border. Use nylon thread in a small sharps needle to apply the beads.

- Starting at the centre point of one border, stitch a row of antique beads, side by side, over the line of running stitch (the holes in the beads lie at right angles to the border and the sides of the beads should be just touching each other). Apply beads up to one blossom, working each stitch towards the outside of the border, then stitch back through each bead to the centre point (still stitching towards the outside). Continue applying beads along the line to the other blossom, then stitch back through these beads to the centre point, thus making two stitches in each bead (the best result is obtained by making the first stitch quite long then using the second stitch to accurately position the bead). Work all stitches towards the outside of the border—this will help to keep the beads straight. Repeat for the other side of the border.

3. COUCHED RAYON GIMP OR PERLE 3 THREAD

A length of variegated viscose gimp is couched on both sides of the row of beads. If gimp is not available, a length of perle 3 thread may be substituted.

- Using one strand of caramel rayon machine thread in a sharps needle, couch a row of plum-caramel gimp (or perle thread) next to the row of beads, working the couching stitches towards and slightly under the beads and 2–3 mm apart. Sink the tails of gimp through to the back, close to the beaded blossoms, with a large yarn darner. Trim the tails and secure. Couch a row of gimp on both sides of the row of beads, working all stitches towards the beads.

4. COUCHED GILT SUPER PEARL PURL

A length of super pearl purl, couched next to the inner row of gimp, forms the inside row of the border.

- Using one strand of fine gold metallic thread (pulled through beeswax) in a size 9 sharps needle, couch a length of super pearl purl next to the inner row of gimp, working the couching stitches towards the gimp. To start, trim one end of purl and place the cut end next to a beaded blossom. Couch the purl in place, one stitch between every second or third coil, pulling the thread down firmly between the coils of purl. Just before the end of the row is reached, cut the purl to the correct length then couch into place.

5. COUCHED GILT NO. 3 PEARL PURL

A length of stretched no. 3 pearl purl, couched next to the outer row of gimp, forms the outside row of the border.

- Cut a 14 cm (5½ in) length of gilt no. 3 pearl purl and stretch to 28 cm (11 in) by holding a coil of purl at each end and pulling apart gently. Cut the stretched purl in half (one piece for each side of the border).

- Using one strand of fine gold metallic thread, couch a length of stretched purl next to the outer row of gimp, working the couching stitches towards the gimp. To start, trim one end of purl and place the cut end next to a beaded blossom. Couch the purl in place, one stitch between every second or third coil. Just before the end of the row is reached, cut the purl to the correct length then couch into place.

6. STITCHED PETITE BEADS

A row of evenly spaced purple/burgundy petite beads is stitched outside the solid border.

With nylon thread in a small sharps needle, stitch a purple/burgundy petite bead at every dot, two stitches per bead and working in a 'back stitch' motion (the hole in the bead is parallel to the border).

7. BEADED BLOSSOM CORNERS

A beaded blossom is stitched in each corner of the panel. If working a book cover, the raised beads help to protect the embroidery.

- Work a beaded prunus blossom over the dots in each corner of the panel, using a 2.5 mm gold bead for the centre and applying eight antique beads (3036) around the outside edge for the petals.

- Apply eight petite beads (40374) around the outside edge of the blossom, one bead at each gap between the antique bead petals.
  Work two stitches in each petite bead, the hole in the bead parallel to the edge of the blossom.

TO COMPLETE THE BOOK COVER

The seams may be stitched by machine or hand using dark cream sewing thread.

1. Remove the fabrics from the hoop and press the edges carefully on the calico side. Check the original outlines and redraw if necessary.

2. Cut the calico (and the silk) along the upper, lower and side outlines of the book cover. To reduce bulk, cut the calico away from the inside covers, cutting close to the line of running stitches along the fold lines (retain the running stitches at this stage).

3. Press under a 1 cm (⅜ in) turning at each side edge of the inside cover and stitch (or fuse).

4. Fold the inside covers along the fold lines, right sides facing, then pin the raw edges together across the top and bottom of the book cover (check the fit of the cover with your book before you stitch).

5. To line the spine of the book cover, cut a piece of silk, 6 x 14.3 cm (2 ⅜ x 5 ⅝ in) from the top edge remnant. Place the lining over the spine space, top and bottom edges even, making sure the sides of the lining overlap the edges of the inside covers. Pin in place.

6. With the calico side up, stitch a 1 cm (⅜ in) seam across the upper and lower edges of the book cover, either by machine or by hand (back stitch), using dark cream sewing thread. To reduce bulk, cut the calico seam allowance away, close to the stitching and trim one of the silk seam allowances to 5 mm (1/4 in) . A narrow ribbon can be sewn in the top seam as a bookmark if desired.

7. Turn the book cover to the right side, making sure the lining is under the edges of the inside cover. Carefully ease out the corners and finger press the seam allowance. Remove any silk running stitches that remain.

8. If desired a wedge of fusible pellon (ogive shaped) may be fused to the front cover of the diary to pad the iris segment. This is optional.

9. Carefully ease the covers of the diary into the book cover.

Cherry Flower Roundel

The colours and design of this small roundel were inspired

by an eighteenth century Mughal enamelled gold vessel, embellished

with stylised cherry-red flowers. Combining stumpwork, goldwork

and surface embroidery techniques, this circular panel is worked on

an ivory satin background with silks, gold metallic threads, beads

and tiny spangles. The design features a variation of the pear flowers

found in the Syrian Pomegranate Tile, and is enclosed by

an ornate border worked in gold metallic threads and beads.

The roundel may be framed, or inserted into the base of a glass

paperweight, or mounted into the lid of a gilt bowl or box.

SPITTOON

India (Rajasthan), eighteenth century

This spitton is a superb example of Mughal jewellers expertise in combining Indian and Western
traditions of goldworking and enamelling. The typically Mughal decoration of stylised red
flowers on a white ground was the inspiration for the Cherry Flower Roundel.

CHERRY FLOWER ROUNDEL DIAGRAM
drawing actual size

Skeleton outline

Detached
flower petal

CHERRY FLOWER ROUNDEL
❧ REQUIREMENTS ❧

This is the complete list of requirements for this embroidery

✣ ivory satin background fabric: 20 cm (8 in) square
✣ quilter's muslin: three 20 cm (8 in) squares

✣ 13 cm (5 in) embroidery hoop
✣ 10 cm (4 in) embroidery hoop
✣ needles:
✣ crewel/embroidery size 10
✣ sharps sizes 9 and 12
✣ sharp yarn darners sizes 14–18
✣ beeswax
✣ embroidery equipment

✣ green stranded thread (stems, leaves): Soie d'Alger 1826 or DMC 500
✣ cherry red stranded thread (flowers, buds): Soie d'Alger 1016 or DMC 321

- ✛ Japanese gold T70
- ✛ gilt 3-ply twist
- ✛ gilt no. 6 smooth passing thread
- ✛ gilt no. 2 pearl purl
- ✛ fine gold metallic thread: YLI 601 Metallic Thread col. gold
- ✛ fine gold silk thread: YLI silk stitch 50 col. 79
- ✛ nylon clear thread: Madeira Monofil 60 col. 1001

- ✛ Mill Hill glass seed beads 02090 (purple)
- ✛ Mill Hill petite beads 42028 (ginger)
- ✛ 2 mm gold beads
- ✛ 2 mm gold spangles

- ✛ 33 gauge white covered wire: fifteen 9 cm (3½ in) lengths (colour carmine if desired, COPIC R37 Carmine)

CHERRY FLOWER ROUNDEL
❧ PREPARATION ❧

Mount the satin background fabric and one piece of muslin for
the backing into the 13 cm (5 in) embroidery hoop.

Trace the skeleton outline on to the muslin backing fabric
(the lines dividing the border into segments would show if the
design were traced to the front).

Using gold silk thread in a small sharps needle, thread trace
the design lines to the front by working a row of running stitches
(from the back) along the stem and leaf outlines and both border
lines, making one long straight stitch at each segment line across
the border (these divide the border into twenty equal segments
and will be removed once the border is complete). As the
design will be embroidered over these running stitches,
they need to be quite small and accurate.

Stems

Using one strand of green thread, couch a double row of Japanese gold thread along all flower stem lines (working the centre flower first), then a single strand along both bud stem lines, working the stitches 2–3 mm apart. Begin by sinking the tails of gold thread through to the back at the edge of the specified flower or bud (or start with a fold for the doubled gold thread), then couch along the stem line towards the base of the design, sinking the tails of gold thread as required. Trim and secure all tails of thread to the backing fabric.

Leaves

With one strand of green thread, outline the leaves in split stitch then work a few padding stitches. Embroider each leaf in satin stitch, working the stitches at an angle across the leaf and enclosing the outline.

Cherry Flowers

Work as for the pear flowers in the Syrian Pomegranate Tile with the following variations. For diagrams and more detailed instructions see pages 142–143.

DETACHED PETALS

1. Mount a square of muslin into a 10 cm (4 in) hoop and trace ten petal outlines (fifteen detached petals are required—work the remaining five petals on the remaining square of muslin).

2. Using one strand of red thread, couch wire around the petal outline, leaving two wire tails at the base that touch but do not cross. Buttonhole stitch the wire to the fabric, then work a row of split stitch inside the wire (as the petals are outlined in buttonhole stitch, they will overlap each other slightly when they are applied, unlike the Pear Flowers).

3. Using a new length of thread, embroider the petals in padded satin stitch, working the stitches towards the base of the petal (make every alternate stitch slightly shorter so that they fan inside the shape). Cut out the petals.

TO COMPLETE CHERRY FLOWER

1. Using a large yarn darner, insert the tails of five petals through a circle of five individual holes (as close to each other as possible). Bend the wire tails back underneath each petal and secure (do not cut the wire tails until the centre is worked).

2. Using tweezers, shape the petals, pushing them gently towards the centre (they will slightly overlap each other). Using nylon thread, sew a 2 mm gold bead into the centre of the flower. Stitch a ginger petite bead (42028) at the base of every petal, carefully bringing the needle out through the petal (from the back) and stitching towards the gold bead (make two stitches in each bead). After a final shaping of the petals, trim the wire tails (shorter than the span of the flower).

Buds

1. With one strand of red thread, outline the bud in split stitch. Work several long chain stitches, inside the outline, to pad the bud.

2. Embroider the bud in satin stitch, enclosing the outline.

3. Using one strand of green thread, cover the base of the bud with slanted straight stitches, worked alternately from the right then the left (a variation of fishbone stitch), starting halfway up the side of the bud and taking the stitches over the lower edge.

Border & Spangles

The outer edges of the border are worked over the two lines of running stitch it is not necessary to remove these stitches. The inside of the border is divided into segments by twenty equally spaced straight stitches—these will be removed when the border is complete.

INNER BORDER LINE

Couch 30 cm (12 in) lengths of Japanese gold thread and gilt 3 ply twist together over the inner line (Japanese gold on the inside), using waxed, fine gold metallic thread in a size 9 sharps needle. Work the couching stitches 2–3 mm apart over both threads. Sink the tails of both gold threads after the couching is complete, and secure.

OUTER BORDER LINE

1. Cut an 11 cm (4¼ in) length of gilt no. 2 pearl purl and stretch to 24 cm (9½ in). Using six strands of red thread each 50 cm (20 in) long, carefully wrap the purl between each coil, leaving a 10 cm (4 in) tail of thread at each end (trim the final coil of purl at each end to neaten, if necessary).

2. Using one strand of red thread, couch the wrapped purl over the outer line. To start, sink one tail of wrapping thread (on the line) and hold at the back with masking tape. Work the couching stitches at an angle over the wrapped purl, one stitch every third or fourth coil, bringing the needle up and down on the line (2–3 mm apart). Just before the starting point is reached, unwrap the red thread, cut the purl to the correct length, rewrap the purl and couch to the end of the line, sinking the tail of wrapping thread through to the back. Secure both tails of red thread.

3. Using fine gold metallic thread, couch a length of gilt 3-ply twist along the outside edge of the wrapped purl, working the couching stitches towards the purl (sink the tails at a different point than the tails of red thread).

4. Using nylon thread in a small sharps needle, couch a single strand of

gilt smooth passing in a scallop pattern, between the border lines, using the stitched segment lines as a guide. Work one scallop in each segment, using tweezers to shape the lower point of the scallop. (I couched all the lower points first, then returned to stitch the curved upper edge of each scallop with about five couching stitches.) Sink the tails of gold thread after the couching is complete, then secure. Remove the silk segment stitches.

5. Using nylon thread, stitch a 2 mm gold bead in the centre of the scallop, the hole in the bead parallel to the border lines. Stitch four purple seed beads around the gold bead (one at each side, one at the top and one at the bottom), working all the stitches towards the central gold bead (make several stitches through each bead—the purple beads need to be as close as possible to the gold bead). Repeat for each scallop.

6. Stitch gold spangles to background with nylon or fine gold metallic thread, making three stitches into each spangle (secure the thread behind each spangle before moving on to the next one).

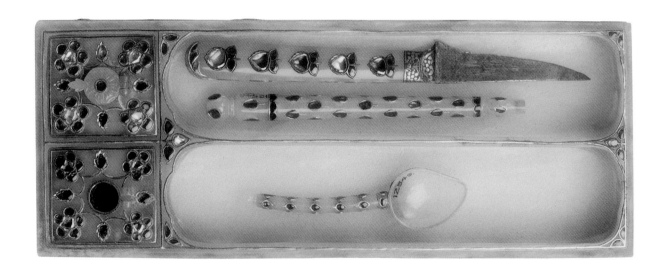

PEN BOX & UTENSILS
Indian (Mughal), eighteenth century

islamic

*Examples of Islamic art may be found in a multitude of forms,
often reflecting the geographical and cultural diversity of the lands of
Islam—from Spain and North Africa in the west to India
and South-east Asia in the east. This section includes projects
inspired not only by ceramic tiles, but also by manuscripts,
textiles, and enamelled gold treasures from Arabia, Tunisia,
Mughal India and the Ottoman Empire.*

Mughal Grapevine Tile

This elegant square panel was inspired by enamelled

gold treasures from the Mughal Empire. Combining goldwork

and surface embroidery techniques, this tile is worked on an ivory

satin background with silks, gold metallic threads, beads and tiny

spangles. The design features a stylised vine, based on the

arabesque, leaves in laid and couched work, and beaded grapes,

all enclosed by an ornate narrow border worked in gold metallic

threads and variegated rayon gimp.

OTTOMAN
SQUARE PANEL

PATTERN FROM A
COTTON-PRINTER'S
BLOCK
Indian, nineteenth century

The Grapevine Tile design is based on the square panel with double-curved, ogee form sides,
a common feature in Islamic design. The lines on which the design of the square is based (the two
diagonals and the two diameters), divide the figure into eight equal spaces which are
decorated with a repeating vine-scroll ornament. The centre of the shape,
where the lines intersect, is accentuated by the leaf 'rosette'.

MUGHAL GRAPEVINE TILE DIAGRAM
drawing actual size

MUGHAL GRAPEVINE TILE
❧ REQUIREMENTS ❧

This is the complete list of requirements for this embroidery

- ✛ ivory satin background fabric: 30 cm (12 in) square
- ✛ calico backing fabric: 30 cm (12 in) square

- ✛ 25 cm (10 in) embroidery hoop or stretcher bars
- ✛ needles:

    crewel/embroidery size 10

    sharps sizes 9 and 12

    chenille sizes 18—22

    sharp yarn darners sizes 14—18
- ✛ beeswax
- ✛ embroidery equipment

- ✛ green stranded thread (leaves): Soie d'Alger 2126 or DMC 3345
- ✛ garnet stranded thread (grapes): Soie d'Alger 4636 or DMC 902

For ease of use, the requirements of each individual element are repeated under its heading—for example, Leaves requirements, Vine requirements.

- ✤ variegated garnet viscose gimp (border): Stef Francis Gimp col. 01 or substitute DMC Perle 3 col. 902 (garnet) and matching stranded thread
- ✤ Madeira Rayon No.40 col. 1358 (closest match to gimp)
- ✤ Japanese gold T69
- ✤ gilt 3-ply twist
- ✤ gold couching thread 371
- ✤ gilt no. 6 smooth passing thread
- ✤ gilt super pearl purl
- ✤ gilt no. 3 pearl purl
- ✤ fine gold metallic thread: YLI 601 Metallic Thread col. gold
- ✤ fine gold silk thread: YLI Silk Stitch 50 col. 79
- ✤ nylon clear thread: Madeira Monofil 60 col. 1001

- ✤ Mill Hill seed beads 00367 (garnet)
- ✤ Mill Hill frosted beads 60367 (garnet)
- ✤ Mill Hill petite beads 40557 (gold)
- ✤ 2 mm gold spangles

MUGHAL GRAPEVINE TILE
❦ PREPARATION ❦

Mount the satin background fabric and the calico backing into
the embroidery hoop or square frame.

Using a fine lead pencil, trace the skeleton outline of the design
onto tracing paper (this is a mirror image of the design). Do not use
too much lead on the vine lines. Turn the tracing paper over and transfer the
skeleton outline to the background fabric with a stylus, taking care to align
the design with the straight grain of the fabric (place a board underneath the
frame of fabric to provide a firm surface). Note: To ensure that the
traced vine lines are not too thick, use a fine stylus (the vine lines
will be covered with only one row of gilt passing thread).

Using gold silk thread in a small sharps needle, work a row of running
stitches along the border line, working a back stitch into each corner to
facilitate the working of the border. As the border threads will be applied over
these running stitches, they need to be quite small and accurate.

Leaves

REQUIREMENTS

✢ green stranded thread: Soie d'Alger 2126 or DMC 3345

✢ gold couching thread 371

✢ nylon clear thread: Madeira Monofil 60 col. 1001 or fine gold metallic thread
(e.g. YLI 601 Metallic Thread col. gold if preferred; I used nylon thread)

1. With one strand of green thread in a crewel needle, cover the surface of the leaf with long satin stitches worked horizontally across the shape. The leaves may also be worked in surface/laid satin stitch (all the long stitches are on the front surface of the work). It is easier to make the first stitch across the centre of the shape (at the widest extremity), then work the satin stitches to the curved top edge of the leaf, then to the lower point.

2. Using nylon thread in a small sharps needle, couch gold couching thread across the surface of the leaf (to form veins) and around the outside edge, as follows:

• With gold couching thread in a chenille needle, make a stitch from 1 to 2, then couch the thread into curved 'veins' with nylon thread.

• Bring the gold thread out at 3 and insert at 4, then bring out again at 3 and insert at 5. Couch the thread into curved 'veins' with nylon thread.

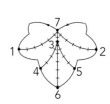

• Bring the gold thread out at 6 then couch along the centre of the leaf to form the central vein.

• Finally, couch the gold thread around the outside edge of the leaf, inserting the tail of gold thread through to the back at 7. Secure and trim.

Panel decorated with arabesque pattern, Persian

Vine

The vine is worked with gilt smooth passing thread, couched in place with nylon (or fine gold metallic) thread. The tile consists of four 'vine' quadrants, each worked the same way. It is advisable to complete one quadrant before proceeding to the next.

REQUIREMENTS

+ gilt no. 6 smooth passing thread
+ nylon clear thread: Madeira Monofil 60 col. 1001 or fine gold metallic thread (e.g. YLI 601 Metallic Thread col. gold; if preferred; I used nylon thread)
+ Mill Hill petite beads 40557 (gold)

1. Using nylon thread in a small sharps needle, couch a row of gilt smooth passing along the curved stem lines between the leaves, in the centre of the tile (I cut separate lengths of gilt thread for each stem). Work the stitches 2–3 mm apart and use a chenille needle to sink the tails of gilt thread through to the back. Secure the tails with a few stitches behind the leaf and trim.

2. Using nylon thread, stitch a gold bead at the top point of the vine (1), with two stitches worked horizontally. Cut 30 cm (12 in) of gilt passing thread and insert one end through this gold bead (the end of the thread can be dipped in PVA glue or nail polish—optional). Pull the gilt thread through until the tails are of equal length. Thread four gold beads onto each tail of thread (one of the tails only requires two beads but it is easier to start with the same number on both sides). Stick a small tab of masking tape to the end of each tail to prevent the beads from sliding off the thread.

3. Commencing at the top gold bead, couch the left tail of gilt thread along the left vine line, continuing on to the right towards (2) and keeping the threaded gold beads out of the way (it is easier to achieve a smooth curve if the couching stitches are worked from the inside of the curve towards the outside). Before (2) is reached, slide a gold bead along the gilt thread and couch in place, just before the point where the vine divides. Continue couching the gilt thread towards (3). Just before stitching the curved tendril at the end of the line, remove the tab of masking tape and excess beads, retaining one bead. Couch the gilt thread to the end of the line, then twist to form a small coil (a yarn darner helps with this). Insert the tail of gilt thread through to the back, adjusting the coil of thread so that the gold bead is in the centre. Couch the coil into place and secure the tail of thread at the back. Trim.

4. To form tendril 4, cut a short length of gilt passing and thread on a gold bead. Sink one tail of thread at (2) then couch the gilt thread along the curved tendril, forming the beaded coil as for (3). Secure threads and trim.

5. Couch a short length of gilt thread along the grape stem (5) inserting the tails through to the back at each end. To facilitate the stitching of the grapes, fold the tail of gilt thread at the 'grape end' back under the stem and secure with a few small stitches.

6. Returning to the top gold bead, couch the right tail of gilt thread along the right vine line, couching a gold bead in place at (6), just after the threads cross. Continue on to the left towards (7), couching a gold bead in place, just before the point where the vine divides. Continue couching the gilt thread towards (8) couching a gold bead in place just before the vine divides. Couch the gilt thread to the end of the line (9), then twist to form a small coil and insert the tail of gilt thread through to the back. Couch the coil and secure the tail of thread. Trim.

7. To form tendril (10), cut a length of gilt passing and thread on a gold bead. Sink one tail of thread at (7) then couch the gilt thread along the curved tendril, forming the beaded coil as for (3). Secure threads and trim.

8. To form tendril (11), cut a short length of gilt passing and thread on a gold bead. Sink one tail of thread at (8) then couch the gilt thread along the curved tendril, forming the beaded coil as for (3). Secure threads and trim.

9. Couch a short length of gilt thread along the grape stem as for (5).

10. Cut a 15 cm (6 in) length of gilt passing and thread on two gold beads. Sink one tail of thread at (6), then couch the gilt thread along the line towards (12), couching a gold bead in place, just before the point where the vine divides. Couch the gilt thread to the end of the line (13), then twist to form a small coil and insert the tail of gilt thread through to the back. Couch the coil into place and secure the tail of thread at the back. Trim.

11. Couch a length of gilt thread along the grape stem as for (5).

Repeat for the remaining three quadrants of the tile.

Grapes

The grapes are worked with wine coloured beads, stitched in rows over thread padding.

REQUIREMENTS

- garnet stranded thread: Soie d'Alger 4636 or DMC 902
- Mill Hill seed beads 00367 (garnet)
- Mill Hill frosted beads 60367 (garnet)

PADDING

Using six strands of thread in a chenille needle, work the padding for the grapes as follows:

1. Work a straight stitch from A to B.

2. Work a detached chain stitch around the straight stitch with the anchoring stitch close to B.

3. Work a second detached chain stitch around the first.

4. Work a long straight stitch from C to D.

5. With one strand of thread, work three horizontal couching stitches across the padding (do not pull too tight).

Note: Cross the tails of padding thread behind the shape and hold out of the way with masking tape. Trim the tails of padding thread after the beads have been applied.

BEADED GRAPES

The grapes are formed by stitching rows of beads across the padding, working a couching stitch between each bead. Use a mixture of the beads for each bunch of grapes (e.g. twelve frosted beads and eleven shiny seed beads), then select at random when applying. Use one strand of garnet thread in a crewel needle.

Row 1: Bring the needle out on one side of the padding, just below the stem end of the grapes (D), and thread on three beads. Insert the needle on the other side of the padding then work a couching stitch between each bead.

Row 2: Bring the needle out below the previous row of beads, 1 mm away from the edge of the padding. Thread on five beads then insert the needle on the other side of the padding, 1 mm away from the edge. Work a couching stitch between each bead. For best results, couch on either side of the centre bead first, then work the couching stitches on either side, angling all stitches towards the centre.

Row 3: Apply five beads as above.

Row 4: Apply four beads, working the first couching stitch between the two centre beads.

Row 5: Apply three beads.

Row 6: Apply two beads—these beads should cover the lower end of the padding.

Row 7: Finally, stitch one bead at the lower end to complete the bunch of grapes.

Border & Spangles

REQUIREMENTS

- variegated garnet viscose gimp: Stef Francis Gimp col. 01
  or substitute DMC Perle 3 col. 902 (garnet) and matching stranded thread
- Madeira Rayon No.40 col. 1358 (closest match to gimp)
- Japanese gold T69
- gilt 3-ply twist
- gilt super pearl purl
- gilt no. 3 pearl purl
- fine gold metallic thread: Madeira Metallic 9803 col. 3007
- fine gold silk thread: YLI Silk Stitch 50 col. 79
- nylon clear thread: Madeira Monofil 60 col. 1001
- 2 mm gold spangles

Five rows of assorted threads and wires are couched side by side to produce a narrow solid border, using the outline of running stitch as a guide to placement.

Starting from the inside border line these rows comprise:

Row A: couched Super Pearl Purl.

Row B: couched Japanese Gold thread.

Row C: couched variegated Viscose Gimp
(or garnet coloured Perle thread).

Row D: couched Gilt 3-ply Twist.

Row E: couched Gilt No. 3 Pearl Purl.

Work the border in the following order.

1. VARIEGATED GARNET VISCOSE GIMP (ROW C)

Using one strand of rayon thread, couch a row of variegated garnet gimp over the line of running stitches to form the centre row of the border. (Substitute DMC Perle 3 col. 902 garnet if the gimp is not available.) Work the stitches 2–3 mm apart and sink the tails of gimp through to the back at one corner. Secure and trim.

2. JAPANESE GOLD THREAD (ROW B)

Using waxed fine gold metallic thread in a size 9 sharps needle, couch a length of Japanese gold thread inside the row of couched gimp, working the couching stitches towards and slightly under the gimp, 2–3 mm apart, and in a brick pattern. Sink the tails of Japanese gold thread through to the back at another corner. Secure and trim.

3. GILT 3-PLY TWIST (ROW D)

Using fine gold metallic thread, couch a length of gilt twist on the outside of the row of couched gimp, working the couching stitches towards and slightly under the gimp, 2–3 mm apart, and in a brick pattern (the couching stitches may be worked diagonally, following the angle of the twist). Sink the tails of gilt twist through to the back at one of the side indentations (this gives a neater result than sinking at a corner). Secure and trim.

4. COUCHED GILT SUPER PEARL PURL (ROW A)

Using one strand of waxed fine gold silk thread, couch a length of super pearl purl next to the row of Japanese gold thread to form the inside row of the border. Trim one end of the purl (to neaten) then, starting inside one corner, couch the purl in place, one stitch between every second or third coil, working the couching stitches towards the Japanese gold Pull the thread down firmly between the coils of purl and carefully bend the purl into points to work the corners. Just before the starting corner is reached, cut the purl to the correct length then couch into place.

5. COUCHED GILT NO. 3 PEARL PURL (ROW E)

Cut a 30 cm (12 in) length of gilt no. 3 pearl purl and stretch to 60 cm (24 in) by holding a coil of purl at each end and pulling apart gently.

Using nylon thread (or fine gold metallic thread), couch a length of stretched purl next to the row of gilt twist to form the outside row of the border, carefully bending the purl around the corner points. Trim one end of the purl (to neaten) then, starting at one of the side indentations (not at a corner), couch the purl in place, one stitch between every coil, working the couching stitches towards the twist. Just before the starting point is reached, cut the purl to the correct length then couch into place, tails of purl abutting at the indentation.

6. SPANGLES

Using the photograph as a guide to placement, stitch gold spangles to the background with nylon or fine gold metallic thread, making three stitches into each spangle.

Ottoman Tulip Panel

Inspired by Turkish enamelled wall-tiles, this small ornate

embroidery features the tulips and colours so beloved of the

Ottomans. Combining stumpwork, goldwork and surface embroidery

techniques, the panel is worked on an ivory satin background with

silks, gold metallic threads, beads and tiny spangles. Embroidered in

the characteristic palette of rich coral orange (known as

'Armenian bole'), cobalt blue and dark sage green, the design

features tulips with detached petals, and beaded prunus blossoms,

all enclosed in a stylised palmette border.

BORDERS OF TURKISH TILES

The design outline of the Ottoman Tulip Panel is a variation of the palmette knop shape,
a foliated form common in Islamic designs, as shown in these panels of tiles.

OTTOMAN TULIP PANEL DIAGRAMS
drawings actual size

Skeleton outline

Detached tulip
petal outline

Tulip side petals
padding outlines

OTTOMAN TULIP PANEL
❧ REQUIREMENTS ❧

This is the complete list of requirements for this embroidery

- ✛ ivory satin background fabric: 20 cm (8 in) square
- ✛ quilter's muslin (or calico) backing fabric: 20 cm (8 in) square
- ✛ quilter's muslin: 15 cm (6 in) square
- ✛ red felt: 5 x 8 cm (2 x 3 in)
- ✛ paper-backed fusible web: 5 x 8 cm (2 x 3 in)

- ✛ 15 cm (6 in) embroidery hoop or stretcher bars
- ✛ 10 cm (4 in) embroidery hoop
- ✛ needles:
    crewel/embroidery size 10
    sharps sizes 9 and 12
    chenille sizes 18-22
    sharp yarn darners sizes 14–18
- ✛ beeswax
- ✛ embroidery equipment

- ✛ green stranded thread (stems, leaves): Soie d'Alger 146 or DMC 500
- ✛ dark orange stranded thread (tulips): Soie d'Alger 635 or DMC 900
- ✛ medium orange stranded thread (tulips): Soie d'Alger 645 or DMC 946
- ✛ cobalt blue stranded thread (tulips, border): Soie d'Alger 116 or DMC 820

- ✛ Japanese gold T70
- ✛ gilt no. 6 smooth passing thread
- ✛ gilt super pearl purl
- ✛ fine gold metallic thread: YLI 601 Metallic Thread col. gold
- ✛ fine gold silk thread: YLI Silk Stitch 50 col. 79
- ✛ nylon clear thread: Madeira Monofil 60 col. 1001
- ✛ red sewing thread: Gutermann Polyester col. 365

- ✛ Mill Hill seed beads 00020 (cobalt blue)
- ✛ 2.5 mm gold bead
- ✛ 2 mm gold beads
- ✛ 2 mm gold spangles

- ✛ 33 gauge white covered wire: three 12 cm (5 in) lengths
  (colour wire orange if desired, Copic YR07 Cadmium Orange)

OTTOMAN TULIP PANEL
❧ PREPARATION ❧

Mount the satin background fabric and the muslin backing
into the 15 cm (6 in) embroidery hoop.

Using a fine lead pencil, trace the skeleton outline of the design
onto tracing paper. Turn the tracing paper over and transfer the
skeleton outline to the background fabric with a stylus, taking
care to align the design with the straight grain of the fabric (place
a board underneath the frame of fabric to provide a firm surface).

Using gold silk thread in a small sharps needle, work a row of
running stitches along the border line, working a back stitch into
each corner to facilitate the working of the border.
As the border threads will be applied over these running
stitches, they need to be quite small and accurate.

Stems

Using one strand of green thread in a crewel needle, couch a double row of Japanese gold thread along the tulip stem lines, working the centre stem first and making the stitches 2–3 mm apart. Begin by sinking the tails of gold thread through to the back at the lower edge of the tulip outline, then couch along the stem line towards the base of the design, sinking the tails of gold thread as required. Secure all tails of thread at the back, behind the stem.

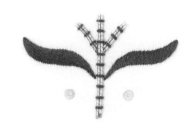

Leaves

With one strand of green thread in a crewel needle, outline the leaves in split stitch then work a few padding stitches. Embroider each leaf in satin stitch, working the stitches at an angle across the leaf and enclosing the outline.

Tulips

The method for working these tulips is similar to that used for the peony buds in the Persian Peony Tile (see pages 82–83).

BACKGROUND PETALS

The background petals for each tulip comprise three petals embroidered on the satin and two padded side petals.

1. Trace three pairs of side petals onto paper-backed fusible web (one pair for each tulip), fuse to red felt and cut out. Using red sewing thread, apply the petal shapes (web side down) over the side petal outlines on the background fabric with small close stab stitches.

2. Using one strand of medium orange thread in a crewel needle, work the outlines of the three upper background petals in back stitch. Embroider the petals in long and short stitch, enclosing the outlines and working the segment at the base of the centre petal in cobalt blue if desired (it will not be seen).

3. Using nylon thread in a small sharps needle, couch a row of gilt smooth passing thread around the edges of the side petals, sinking the tails at the lower points (•) near the stem. Leave a small space at the top of the stem to insert the detached petal.

4. Couch gilt smooth passing thread around the edges of the upper three petals, outlining the centre petal first. Sink the tails of gilt thread at the edges of the centre and side petals (•).

5. With dark orange thread, embroider the side petals in long and short stitch, inside the gilt outline, leaving a small segment at the lower edge of each petal which is worked in cobalt blue thread.

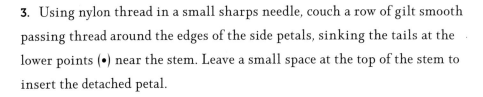

The first Western travellers marvelled that the Ottomans so loved these 'red lilies' that they often wore a single tulip in their turbans, like a plumed aigrette. *Philippa Scott, Turkish Delights, page 28*

DETACHED PETALS

1. Mount muslin into a 10 cm (4 in) hoop and trace three detached tulip petals. Using dark orange thread, couch wire around the petal outline, leaving two wire tails at the base that touch but do not cross. Buttonhole stitch the wire to the fabric then embroider the petal in long and short stitch, working the centre segment in cobalt blue thread.

2. With nylon thread in a small sharps needle, couch gilt smooth passing thread around the edge of the petal, leaving two thread tails at the base.

Work the couching stitches into the buttonhole edge, between the wire and the ridge of the buttonhole stitches, with firm stitches 1.5 mm apart. Cut out the petal and shape slightly.

Apply a detached petal over the embroidered background petals by inserting the wire tails through to the back at the base of the tulip, just above the stem, using a large Yarn Darner. Insert the tails of gilt thread through the same hole. Bend wire and thread tails behind the tulip, secure and trim.

Prunus Blossoms

Work as for the prunus blossoms in the Persian Peony Tile with the following variations. For diagrams and more detailed instructions see pages 86–87.

1. Using nylon thread, securely stitch a 2.5 mm gold bead in the centre of the upper blossom (in the border).

2. To form the petals, stitch one cobalt seed bead next to the gold bead (the hole parallel to the edge of the gold bead). Bring the needle to the front, pass it through the cobalt bead then thread on seven more beads. Pass needle through the first bead again, forming a circle of cobalt beads. Take the needle through to the back and bring out on the other side of the circle of beads. Couch between each cobalt bead, then thread the needle through all eight beads several times to pull the beads into an even circle. Secure the thread.

3. Repeat for the remaining three blossoms, applying a 2 mm gold bead for the centres, and seven cobalt beads around the edge for the petals.

Border & Spangles

Three rows of assorted threads and wires are couched side by side to produce a narrow solid border, using the outline of running stitch as a guide to placement. Starting from the inside, the rows are:

Row 1: couched Japanese gold threads.

Row 2: couched cobalt blue wrapped pearl purl.

Row 3: couched Japanese gold thread

Work the border in the following order.

1. JAPANESE GOLD THREAD

Using fine gold metallic thread in a size 9 sharps needle, couch a double row of Japanese gold thread (two 60 cm lengths) over the line of running stitch to form the inside row of the border. Work the couching stitches 2 mm apart over both threads except at the corners of the indentations, where each thread is first couched individually, then a stitch is worked over both, to achieve a sharper point. Sink the tails of Japanese gold thread through to the back at a lower corner. Secure and trim.

2. WRAPPED PEARL PURL

- Cut a 25 cm (10 in) length of gilt super pearl purl and stretch to 50 cm (20 in) by holding a coil of purl at each end and pulling apart gently. Trim ends to neaten.

- Using three strands of cobalt blue thread each 70 cm (28 in) long, carefully wrap the extended purl between each coil, leaving a tail of thread at each end.

- Using one strand of cobalt blue thread in a crewel needle, couch the wrapped purl outside the Japanese gold thread, carefully bending into shape at the corners with tweezers. To start, sink one tail of wrapping thread inside a lower corner and hold at the back with masking tape. Work the couching stitches at an angle over the wrapped purl (stitching towards the Japanese gold), one stitch every second or third coil and working a couching stitch at each corner. Just before the end of the line is reached (the starting point), unwrap the cobalt blue thread, cut the purl to the correct length, rewrap the purl and couch to the end of the line, sinking the tail of wrapping thread through to the back (next to the starting point). Secure the tails of wrapping thread and trim.

3. JAPANESE GOLD THREAD

Using nylon thread in a small sharps needle, couch a single row of Japanese gold thread next to the row of wrapped purl to form the outside of the border. Starting inside a lower corner, work the couching stitches 2 mm apart and at each corner and indentation. Sink the tails of Japanese gold thread through to the back, secure and trim.

SPANGLES

Stitch gold spangles to background with nylon or fine gold metallic thread, making three stitches into each spangle (secure the thread behind each spangle before moving on to the next one).

Tulips had been cultivated in Turkey for 500 years before becoming a staple of Ottoman design. By the end of the sixteenth century, they had been introduced to Europe, leading in the 1630s to 'Tulipmania', a wild bubble of speculation in bulbs by the Dutch.
Islamic Art in Detail, page 80 - The British Museum

Or Nué Tunisian Palace

The elaborate buildings featured in this small square

panel were inspired by a map of the North African city of

al-Mahdiyah in Ifriqiya (modern-day Tunisia), contained in an

eleventh century manuscript, *The Book of Curiosities of the Sciences and*

Marvels for the Eyes. Using the goldwork technique or nué, this exotic

tile is worked on firm calico with gold metallic thread, fine silks and

cottons. The completed embroidery may be framed, inserted

into the lid of a box or made into a brooch.

MEDIEVAL ISLAMIC VIEWS OF THE COSMOS
The Book of Curiosities

Visiting the Bodleian Library in Oxford, I came across a small image of
three medieval harbour buildings from al-Mahdiyah. I just had to embroider them!
On further investigation I found that they came from a map contained in a recently
discovered manuscript, loosely translated as The Book of Curiosities of the Sciences
and Marvels for the Eyes, acquired by the Bodleian Library in 2002. This previously
unknown Arabic treatise on cosmography is a late twelfth or early thirteenth century
copy of an anonymous work assembled in the first half of the eleventh century in Egypt.
It contains a remarkable series of astronomical diagrams and early maps, of which one
was the source of the images of the palaces. The map which inspired this embroidery
can be found in Book 2, Chapter 13: On the peninsula of al-Mahdiyah.

This chapter includes a textual description of the city, followed by a map.
The text of the chapter describes the foundation of the city by the Fatimid caliphs in
916–921, as well as its subsequent siege by the forces of the Kharijite rebel known as 'the
Man on the Donkey'. The map depicts the city in bird's-eye view, as seen
from the south-west, and surrounded by stone walls. In the south-eastern
corner is the entrance to the enclosed inner harbour. Two isolated and
rather elaborate buildings are the palaces of the rulers.

Emilie Savage-Smith and Yossef Rapoport (eds), The Book of Curiosities: A Critical Edition.
World-Wide-Web publication (www.bodley.ox.ac.uk/bookofcuriosities) (March 2007).

OR NUÉ TUNISIAN PALACES
❧ REQUIREMENTS ❧

This is the complete list of requirements for this embroidery

✢ firm unwashed calico/cotton fabric: 20 cm (8 in) square

✢ slate or square frame or 15 cm (6 in) embroidery hoop bound with tape

....

✢ fine brown waterproof marking pen
(I used a brown Pigma Micron 01 pen)

✢ paints, felt-tip pens (e.g. Copic markers) or coloured pencils

✢ small ruler

....

✢ needles:
sharps size 9 and 12
chenille sizes 18–22

✢ beeswax

✢ embroidery equipment

✛ gilt no. 6 smooth passing thread

✛ fine gold metallic thread: YLI 601 Metallic Thread col. gold

✛ red stranded thread: Needlepoint Inc. Silk col. 448 Persimmon Red

✛ orange stranded thread: Weeks Dye Works col. 2268 Fire

✛ yellow stranded thread: Threadworks col. 1072 Wild Poppies

✛ dark purple stranded thread: Needlepoint Inc. Silk col. 606 Soft Mauve

✛ medium purple stranded thread: Weeks Dye Works col. 1316 Mulberry

✛ green stranded thread: Needlepoint Inc. Silk col. 403 Forest Green

✛ fine black silk thread: Pearsall's Black Work Silk Fine
    or YLI Silk Thread #100

Note: I used a variety of stranded silk and cotton threads, often overdyed or variegated, to obtain the effect that I wanted. Variegated thread is useful in or nué as you can change the shading of the colours that you are using without having too many threads and needles on the go. You may substitute any threads and colours that you like, bearing in mind that thinner threads are easier to work with than thicker threads.

OR NUÉ TUNISIAN PALACES DIAGRAM
drawing actual size

OR NUÉ TUNISIAN PALACES
❧ PREPARATION ❧

Mount the calico in a square frame (or embroidery hoop),
making sure that the fabric is drum tight and that the grain of the
fabric remains straight.

Trace the design outline onto tracing paper with a sharp
lead pencil then flip the paper over and draw over the outline on the
back. Turn the tracing paper back to the right side then transfer the
outline to the calico with a stylus, taking care to align the design
with the straight grain of the fabric (place a board underneath
the fabric to provide a firm surface).

Draw over the design outlines with a fine marking pen.
Using paint, marking pens or pencils, colour in the interior shapes
of the buildings, using the photograph as a guide. Colour the
background of the calico with gold-coloured paint or marking pen
if desired. With a sharp lead pencil, rule horizontal lines across the
calico, approximately 5 mm (¼ in) apart (use these to help keep the
rows of couched gilt thread straight).

The Tunisian Palaces have been worked

in the goldwork technique of or nué, regarded as the supreme example of the embroiderer's art in the thirteenth and fourteenth centuries.

A very time-consuming technique, or nué had its origins in Europe, where it was used to work ecclesiastical vestments and hangings. It is a method of couching gold thread across a design drawn or painted on a firm background fabric, the aim being to cover the surface with rows of perfectly straight, couched gold threads (usually in pairs) with no background fabric showing through.

Couching stitches, worked in coloured silk or cotton threads, pick out the design lines, the shading of the design depending on the closeness and/or the colour of the couching stitches, while the areas to remain gold (usually the background) are couched in fine gold thread.

TO WORK THE TUNISIAN PALACES IN OR NUÉ

Use the following instructions to stitch rows of double gilt passing thread to completely cover the surface of the panel.

1. Starting at the bottom line of the design square, couch consecutive rows of double gilt passing thread to the calico, over the painted design, to completely cover the surface. Work the couching stitches in each row with either gold metallic thread or coloured stranded thread, using the design painted on the background fabric as a guide (the first few rows and the last few rows will be couched with gold metallic thread only).

- Use one strand of either silk, cotton or gold metallic thread to work the couching stitches, and a separate needle for each thread—a size 9 sharps needle for the gold metallic thread and size 12 sharps needles for the stranded silks and cottons. Pull the gold metallic thread through beeswax to help prevent shredding.

- Use gold metallic thread to couch the background of the design, working the stitches 2–3 mm apart in a brick pattern.

- Use coloured thread to couch the buildings with close, vertical couching stitches, referring to the colour painted on the calico. Use separate threads and needles for each block of colour. It may be necessary to work some of the coloured stitches at an angle to follow the design.

- Work all the couching stitches in each row before proceeding to the row above, keeping all needles and tails of thread at the front of the work to prevent tangles on the back. Leave 5 cm (2 in) tails of gilt passing thread at either side of the square outline—these are taken through to the back when the couching is finished (hold the tails out of the way with masking tape).

- Use the drawn horizontal lines to help keep the rows of gilt passing thread straight and parallel. As the work progresses, the coloured couching stitches tend to force the rows apart a little, resulting in tiny gaps between the rows of gold-couched background threads. The gold-painted background fabric helps disguise these gaps.

2. When the couching is complete, work the building outlines and internal lines in back stitch and straight stitches with one strand of fine black thread, using the photograph as a guide (take care not to pierce the gilt thread).

3. Sink all tails of passing thread through to the back, using a chenille needle. Secure and trim. The finished panel may be framed or made into a brooch or box top. I laced my panel over a 5.2 x 4.8 cm (2 x 1 $^7/_8$ in) padded cardboard shape and inserted it into a paper-covered cardboard frame. I then made it into a brooch.

Arabian Border

This colourful border was inspired by the exquisite examples of early Arabian art used to ornament the window surrounds in the interior of the ninth century Mosque of Ibn Tulun, Cairo. Employing appliqué and surface embroidery techniques, this border is worked on a charcoal-grey silk background with cottons, gold metallic threads, beads and small pieces of silk fabric.

The design features a stylised vine, made from twisted cord, enclosing floral and heart shaped applied motifs, surrounded by narrow rows of silk ribbon and gold metallic thread. The border may be used to frame a special photograph or memento. I designed the border to enclose a small stumpwork figure, the Chief Eunuch from the ballet Scheherazade, in a costume from Diaghilev's Ballets Russes. Scheherazade was the storyteller of the Tales of the Arabian Nights, or One Thousand and One Nights, which includes the stories of Sinbad, Ali Baba and Aladdin. The instructions for the Chief Eunuch are not provided, however, you may choose to create your own stumpwork figure.

ARABIAN BORDER OUTLINE DIAGRAM
drawing actual size

Skeleton outline

ARABIAN BORDER DIAGRAMS
drawings actual size

corner flower shapes

Central petal
shape

Side petals
silk shapes

Side petals
padding shapes

flower bud shapes

Flower bud
shape

Detached leaf
outlines

Heart padding
shape

Heart silk
shape

ARABIAN BORDER
❧ REQUIREMENTS ❧

This is the complete list of requirements for this embroidery

- ✛ charcoal silk background fabric (or fabric of choice): 40 cm (16 in) square
- ✛ calico backing fabric: 40 cm (16 in) square
- ✛ dark green silk (firm weave like taffeta): 20 cm (8 in) square
- ✛ fusible non-woven interfacing (Vilene): two 20 cm (8 in) squares
- ✛ quilter's muslin: 20 cm (8 in) square (optional)
- ✛ fine red silk: 20 cm (8 in) square
- ✛ orange/yellow shot silk: 20 cm (8 in) square
- ✛ red felt: 10 x 8 cm (4 x 3 in)
- ✛ paper-backed fusible web: 10 x 8 cm (4 x 3 in)

- ✛ slate or square frame or 30 cm (12 in) embroidery hoop
- ✛ 15 cm (6 in) embroidery hoop
- ✛ needles:
  crewel/embroidery size 10
  sharps sizes 9 and 12
  straw/milliners sizes 3–9
  chenille sizes 18–22
  sharp yarn darners sizes 14–18
- ✛ beeswax
- ✛ embroidery equipment

- ✛ dark green stranded thread (vine, leaves): DMC 937
- ✛ orange stranded thread (flowers): DMC 946
- ✛ yellow stranded thread (flowers): DMC 741
- ✛ cobalt blue stranded thread (flowers): DMC 820
- ✛ orange pearl cotton (flowers): DMC Perlé 5 col. 946
- ✛ yellow pearl cotton (flowers): DMC Perlé 5 col. 741

- ✛ Madeira Rayon No. 40 col. 1039 (red)
- ✛ Japanese gold T70
- ✛ gold couching thread 371
- ✛ gold T70 twist (2 x 2)

- ✛ fine gold metallic thread: YLI 601 Metallic Thread col. gold
- ✛ fine gold silk thread: YLI Silk stitch 100 col. 215
- ✛ nylon clear thread: Madeira Monofil 60 col. 1001

- ✛ Mill Hill seed beads 00020 (cobalt blue)
- ✛ 2.5 mm gold beads
- ✛ 4 mm red silk ribbon (Au Ver à Soie col. 940)
- ✛ 33 gauge white covered wire (leaves): twenty 9 cm lengths (colour dark green if desired, Copic G99 Olive)

Page of ornamented architraves and under-surfaces of windows in the interior of the Mosque of Ibn Tulun, Cairo.

ARABIAN BORDER
❧ PREPARATION ❧

Mount the silk background fabric and the
calico backing into the square frame or embroidery hoop.

Using a fine lead pencil, trace the skeleton outline
of the design onto tracing paper.

Tape the tracing, right (pencil) side down, to the calico backing
(check that the design will be on the straight grain of the main fabric).

Draw over all the traced lines with a stylus or used ball-point pen, thus
transferring a pencil outline onto the backing fabric. Optional: Draw over the
pencil lines with a fine marking pen (Pigma), as it tends to fade over time.

Using gold silk thread in a small sharps needle, work a row of running
stitches along the inner border line, the inside line of the outer border and
the vine outline. As the border and vine will be applied over these running
stitches, they need to be quite small and accurate.

The floral and heart motifs will be applied, referring to the outlines
on the back for placement. These outlines may be thread-traced through to
the front, with small running stitches in gold silk thread, if preferred.

Appliquéd Corner Flowers

CENTRE PETAL

1. Trace four centre petal shapes onto Vilene and fuse to the back of the orange/yellow shot silk (the petals for the ten buds may be traced and fused at the same time). Carefully cut out the shapes.

2. Using one strand of gold silk thread in a small sharps needle, appliqué the petal shape to the background fabric with small stab stitches, using the outline on the back as a guide to placement (the stab stitches do not need to be too close together as the raw edge of the silk will be covered by couched pearl cotton).

3. With one strand of yellow stranded thread, couch a row of yellow pearl cotton around the outside edge of the petal (this row is on the background fabric, next to the cut edge of the petal), working the couching stitches towards the petal. Sink the tails of pearl cotton through to the back at the base of the petal • .

4. With one strand of orange stranded thread, couch a row of orange pearl cotton inside the yellow row (covering the edge of the petal). Sink the tails of pearl cotton through to the back at the base of the petal • .

SIDE PETALS

1. Trace four pairs of side petal padding shapes on to paper-backed fusible web (one pair for each corner flower), fuse to red felt and cut out. Cut four pairs of side petal shapes from red silk. Centre a padding shape on the wrong side of one of the side petal silk shapes (the felt may be ironed to the back of the silk as long as the glue does not show through the fine silk fabric—test first). Finger press the turning allowance around the felt padding and stitch temporarily in place with small running stitches using one strand of red rayon thread in a small sharps needle.

Examples of Islamic ornament from Sancta Sophia.

2. Using red rayon thread, appliqué the side petal shapes to the background fabric (over the centre petal) with small stab stitches, using the outline on the back as a guide to placement.

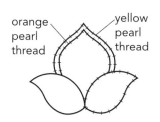

3. With nylon thread in a small sharps needle, couch a row of gold T70 around both side petal shapes, sinking the tails of thread through to the back at the base of the petals. Secure and trim. Remove the red rayon running stitches.

4. Couch a row of gold couching thread, in a figure-of-eight pattern, on top of the silk-covered side petal, using the photograph as a guide. Sink the tails of gold thread through to the back at the base of the petal.

FLOWER CENTRE

Using one strand of cobalt blue thread, work the flower centre outline in back stitch. Stitch cobalt blue beads in the centre of the flower, then work French knots, with two strands of blue thread, to fill any gaps.

Appliquéd Buds

1. Trace ten bud shapes onto Vilene and fuse to the back of the orange/yellow shot silk (if you have not already done so in combination with the centre petals for the four corner flowers). Carefully cut out the shapes.

2. Using one strand of gold silk thread in a small sharps needle, appliqué the bud shape to the background fabric with small stab stitches, using the outline on the back as a guide to placement (the stab stitches do not need to be too close together as the raw edge of the silk will be covered by couched pearl cotton).

3. Two side petals and a centre petal are defined on the appliquéd shape by couching orange or yellow pearl cotton around the petal outlines, using

yellow pearl
thread

orange pearl
thread

the diagram and photograph as a guide. With one strand of orange stranded thread, couch a row of orange pearl cotton around one side petal, covering the cut side edge. Repeat for the other side petal. Sink the tails of pearl cotton through to the back at the base of the petal

4. With one strand of yellow stranded thread, couch a row of yellow pearl cotton around the centre petal outline. Sink the tails of pearl cotton through to the back at the base of the petal .

5. Using two strands of dark green thread in a straw/milliners needle, work a French knot above each petal indentation.

Appliquéd Hearts

1. Trace six heart padding shapes on to paper-backed fusible web, fuse to red felt and cut out. Cut six heart shapes from red silk. Centre a padding shape on the wrong side of one of the heart silk shapes (the felt may be ironed to the back of the silk as long as the glue does not show through the fine silk fabric—test first). Finger press the turning allowance around the felt padding and stitch temporarily in place with small running stitches using one strand of red rayon thread in a small sharps needle.

2. Using red rayon thread, appliqué the heart shapes to the background fabric with small stab stitches, using the outline on the back as a guide to placement.

3. With nylon thread in a small sharps needle, couch a row of gold T70 around the heart shape, sinking the tails of thread through to the back at the indentation at the top of the shape. Secure and trim. Remove the red rayon running stitches.

4. Using nylon thread, couch a scroll pattern in gold couching thread on top of the silk-covered heart shape, using the diagram and photograph as a guide. Sink the tails of gold thread through to the back at the top indentation of the shape. Stitch cobalt blue beads inside the two loops as shown.

Vine

The vine is worked with a twisted cord couched in place over the vine outline.

1. Make a twisted cord as follows:

- Cut 3.6 m (4 yds) of dark green stranded thread (six strands). Tie a loop at each end.

- Loop one end of thread over a hook (or enlist the aid of a friend) and the other end over a pencil. Keeping the thread taut, twist the pencil round and round until the thread begins to twist on itself.

- Holding the twisted thread firmly, fold in half and allow both sides of the thread to twist together. Whip the ends together, then trim off any uneven ends or previous knots. During the entire process the twisted thread must be held under tension to prevent kinks forming in the cord. A small weight may be suspended at the fold to facilitate a smooth twisting process.

2. Using one strand of dark green thread, couch the cord along the vine outline, making invisible couching stitches across the twist of the cord. Note that the cord is folded at the base of the corner flowers and the flower buds to form their stems. Use a large yarn darner to insert the cord through to the back at the corners as required. Secure tails of thread and trim.

small weight may be
suspended at fold

Border

INNER BORDER

Using nylon thread in a small sharps needle, couch a row of gold twist over the inner line of running stitches, working the couching stitches diagonally across the twist of the cord. Sink the tails of gold twist through to the back at one corner using a large yarn darner. Untwist the tails of gold thread (to reduce bulk) before securing to the backing with a few small stitches. Trim.

OUTER BORDER

1. Stitch a row of red silk ribbon around the outside border line, the inside edge of the ribbon next to the row of running stitches. Using red rayon thread in a small sharps needle, apply the ribbon with small stab stitches, 5 mm apart, worked around both edges of the ribbon (the edges will be covered with gold twist). Fold the ribbon diagonally at the corners to form a mitre.

2. Using nylon thread, couch a row of gold twist on either side of the ribbon (covering the edge), working the couching stitches diagonally across the twist of the cord towards the ribbon. Sink the tails of gold thread through to the back as for the inner border.

To Complete Border

DETACHED LEAVES

I worked the detached leaves on green taffeta ribbon, fused to Vilene. Green silk may be substituted or the leaves may be worked on quilter's muslin, embroidering the leaf surface in padded satin stitch. Check that the colour of the thread matches the green fabric.

1. Mount selected fabric into a small embroidery hoop. Trace ten pairs of detached leaves onto the fabric.

2. With one strand of dark green thread, couch wire to the fabric around the leaf outline, leaving two tails of wire at the base. Buttonhole stitch the wire to the background fabric. Carefully cut out the leaves.

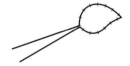

3. Using a large yarn darner, insert the wire tails of the leaves at the base of the bud. Bend the tails behind the bud and secure with a few small stitches. Trim.

GOLD BEADS AND FRENCH KNOTS

1. Using nylon thread, apply gold beads over the dots on either side of the flowers and hearts, using the photograph as a guide and working three or four stitches through each bead.

2. With three strands of dark green thread in a straw/milliners needle, work French knots over the dots at the base of the flower buds and hearts, using the photograph as a guide.

glossary

TECHNIQUES, EQUIPMENT & STITCHES

This section contains general information about the
techniques and equipment that are referred to throughout the book.
The bibliography contains a list of specialised reference books which
can provide more detailed information if required.

Techniques

....

Mounting Fabric
into an embroidery hoop

Good quality embroidery hoops—10 cm, 12 cm, 15 cm, 20 cm and 25 cm (4 in, 5 in, 6 in, 8 in and 10 in)—are essential when working small to medium size designs in stumpwork and goldwork embroidery. Bind the inner ring of wooden hoops with cotton tape to prevent slipping. A small screwdriver is useful to tighten the embroidery hoop. Plastic hoops with a lip on the inner ring are also suitable (because of the lip the inner ring does not need to be bound).

1. Place the main (background) fabric on top of the backing fabric, then place both fabrics over the inner ring of the hoop. If using a plastic hoop, make sure that the lip-edge of the hoop is uppermost.

2. Loosen the outer ring of the hoop so that it just fits over the inner ring and the fabrics, positioning the tension screw at the top of the hoop (12 o'clock). Ease the outer ring down over the inner ring and fabrics.

3. To tension the fabrics in the hoop, pull the fabrics evenly and tighten the screw—alternately—until both layers of fabric are as tight as a drum in the hoop. If using the plastic hoop, the fabric-covered lip-edge of the inner ring should sit just above the top edge of the outer ring. In stumpwork and goldwork, the fabrics are not removed from the hoop until the embroidery is finished.

Mounting Fabric
into square or rectangular frames

A square or rectangular frame is required for larger designs in stumpwork and goldwork embroidery. An artist's stretcher bar frame, a slate frame or a tapestry frame may be used (I use a slate frame).

To Attach the Background and Backing Fabric to a Stretcher Bar Frame

1. Assemble the stretcher bars.

2. Staple or pin (drawing pin/push pin) the background fabric and the calico together to the back of one long side of the frame.

3. Stretch and staple or pin the calico, then the background fabric, to the back of the other long side of the frame (fabrics stretched and secured separately).

4. Staple or pin the background fabric and the calico together to the back of one short side of the frame.

5. Stretch and staple or pin the calico then the background fabric to the back of the remaining short side of the frame.

To Attach the Background and Backing Fabrics to a Slate Frame or Tapestry Frame

1. Select a frame with internal measurements at least 10–15 cm (4–6 in) larger than the required background fabric.

2. To prepare the backing fabric, cut a piece of firm calico or muslin 2 cm (1 in) narrower than the internal width of the frame (the roll bar and webbing) and about 10 cm (4 in) longer than the internal length of the frame. Make sure the fabric is cut on the straight grain.

3. Finish all edges of the calico by first turning under 5 mm (¼ in) then folding over a 1 cm (½ in) hem. Stitch the hem by hand or machine (a length of string may be inserted in the hem of the side edges for extra strength – this is not necessary for smaller embroideries).

4. Mark the centre points of the webbing and calico. With right sides facing and centre points aligned, overcast the top edge of the calico to the webbing edge of one roll bar. Use a double strand of sewing thread and work from the centre point to each end, with the stitches about 5 mm (¼ in) apart. Repeat for the lower roll bar.

5. Assemble the slate frame (or tapestry frame), adjusting the roll bars so that the calico is smooth and taut – not drum tight.

6. Lace the side edges of the calico to the side edges of the frame, using a strong thread (e.g. Cotton Pearl 5 or fine string) still connected to the spool to avoid joins. Make the stitches about 2–3 cm (1 in) apart, leaving a long tail of thread at each end. Adjust the lacing to tighten the calico slightly—not drum tight yet. Secure the ends of the lacing thread temporarily.

7. Centre the background fabric (e.g. silk) over the calico, taking care to align the grains of both fabrics (a little masking tape can be used to hold the silk in place until secured with stitches). With one strand of sewing thread, sew the background fabric to the calico with herringbone stitch, working one edge of the stitch into the background fabric and the other edge into the calico. Start in the centre of the top edge and work to each corner. Repeat for the lower edge, then the sides (do not make the stitches too small or too even.)

8. Tighten the upper and lower bars of the frame, then adjust and secure the lacing on each side so that both layers of fabric are drum tight.

Transferring A Design To Fabric

There are several ways to transfer a design to fabric; choose the most appropriate method for your project.

+ tracing paper (I use GLAD Bake/baking parchment)
+ sharp HB lead pencil (or a 0.5 mm clutch/mechanical pencil)
+ stylus or used ball-point pen (to trace a fine line)
+ masking tape (to stop tracing paper from slipping)
+ tracing board or small, circular lid (use inside the back of the hoop for support when tracing a design on to the front)

PREPARATION

1. Mount the main fabric and a backing fabric (quilter's muslin or calico), into a hoop or square frame. The fabrics need to be kept very taut.

2. Trace the design, either on to the front or to the back, after the fabrics have been mounted into the hoop to prevent distortion.

3. Do not remove the fabrics from the hoop until all the embroidery is finished, unless instructed otherwise.

Tracing the Design onto the Front

Use this method when the traced lines will be completely covered by the embroidery.

1. Trace a skeleton outline of the design onto tracing paper with a sharp lead pencil. Flip the paper over and draw over the outline on the back (do not make the lines too dark).

2. Attach the tracing, right side up, to the fabric in the hoop using strips of masking tape on all sides. Check that the design is on the straight grain of the fabric.

3. Place a tracing board (or lid) inside the back of the hoop for support then transfer the design by tracing over the outline with a stylus, used ball-point pen or a pencil.

Tracing the Design onto the Back

Use this method when the embroidery may not cover the traced lines if they were on the front, or when the main fabric is coloured, patterned or textured. To ensure that your design is the 'right way up' on the main fabric, transfer the skeleton outline to the backing fabric as follows:

1. Trace a skeleton outline of the design onto tracing paper with a sharp lead pencil.

2. Tape the tracing, right (pencil) side down, to the muslin backing (check that the design will be on the straight grain of the main fabric).

3. Draw over all the traced lines with a stylus or used ball-point pen, thus transferring a pencil outline onto the backing fabric. Optional: Draw over the pencil lines with a fine marking pen, as they tend to fade over time (I use light brown Pigma Micron 01).

4. Work by referring to the outline on the back as you stitch. The design lines may be thread-traced through to the front with small running stitches, if required.

Thread-tracing the Design

As this method does not permanently mark the fabric, it offers greater flexibility; however, it is difficult to accurately reproduce fine details of a design.

1. Trace the design on to tissue paper with lead pencil. Place the traced tissue paper over the main fabric and attach to the edges of your frame or hoop with masking tape (check that the design is on the straight grain of the fabric).

2. Using fine silk or machine thread, work small running stitches over the traced lines, through the tissue paper and the fabric. Score the lines with a needle then carefully tear the paper away.

3. Remove the tracing threads as you embroider.

Transferring the Design with a Paper Template

Use this method to achieve very accurate outlines or shapes when pencil lines cannot be used, for example, the centre of the peony (see page 80).

1. Trace the shape on to paper, a removable self-adhesive label, or a Post-it note. Cut out the template and hold in place on the front of the fabric with tacking stitches, if necessary.

2. Work around the template to achieve the desired shape or outline, removing the paper when necessary.

Working With Paper-Backed Fusible Web

Paper-backed fusible web (also known as Vliesofix, Bondaweb and other brand names) is used to fuse or bond one material to another by applying heat with an iron. I also use paper-backed fusible web to obtain a precise design outline on felt—it is very difficult to trace a small shape on to felt and to cut it out accurately!

To Fuse a Design Outline to Felt

1. Trace the outline on to the paper side of the fusible web then fuse to the felt (fusible web/glue side down) with a medium-hot dry iron.

2. Cut out the shape along the outlines. Remove the paper before stitching the felt shape to the background fabric (e.g. flower padding).

Working With Wire

Cake decorator's wire is used to form the detached, wired and embroidered shapes characteristic to stumpwork. I find the following gauges the most useful.

- **30-gauge Covered Wire** This sturdy wire has a tightly-wrapped, thin paper covering and is available in green and white (which can be coloured). It is a strong wire which maintains a shape well when bent—use it for larger detached shapes such as large leaves.

- **33-gauge Covered Wire (Flower Wire)** A fine wire with a tightly-wrapped, thin white paper covering which can be coloured if desired. This wire is used for small, detailed, detached shapes, such as flower petals and narrow leaves.

- **28-gauge Uncovered Wire** Uncovered wire (silver in colour) is used when a finer edge is required—use it for small and detailed detached shapes, wings, antennae and tendrils. Select the 28-gauge uncovered wire as the 30 gauge is a little too thin to retain its shape when stitched.

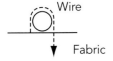

Stitch
Wire
Fabric

Cross section
of fabric, wire
and stitch

To Stitch Wire to Fabric

- When stitching wire to fabric, either with overcast stitch or buttonhole stitch, make sure that the needle enters the fabric at right-angles, very close to the wire (not angled under the wire). The stitches need to be worked very close together, with an up-and-down stabbing motion, using a firm and even tension.

- If you need to renew a thread while stitching wire to fabric, secure the thread tails inside the wired shape (do not use a knot at the edge as it may be cut when cutting out the shape). If you need to renew a thread while stitching wire for a detached shape, you cannot secure the thread inside the wired shape. Instead, hold the tail of the old thread and the tail of the new thread under the length of wire about to be stitched. Catch both tails of thread in with the new overcast stitches.

- When embroidering the veins inside the wings, retain the tails of metallic thread at the front of the wing until it has been cut out, then insert the thread tails through to the back of the wing at the inner corner. When the wings are applied, the thread tails are taken through the main fabric with the tails of wire, and secured at the back.

- Using very sharp scissors with fine points, cut out the wired shape as close to the stitching as possible (stroke the cut edge with your fingernail to reveal any stray threads). If you happen to cut a stitch, use the point of a pin to apply a minute amount of PVA glue to the cut thread. This will dry matt and clear.

To Colour Wire

White, paper-covered wire may be coloured with a waterproof ink or paint if desired. When I colour wires I use Copic Markers which are available from art supply stores. These markers are fast-drying and refillable and come in a huge range of colours.

To Attach Wired Shapes to a Background Fabric

Detached wire shapes are applied to a background fabric by inserting the wire tails through a 'tunnel' formed by the eye of a large (size 14) yarn darner.

1. Pierce the background fabric at the required point with the yarn darner and push it through until the eye of the needle is half-way through the fabric (this forms a 'tunnel' through to the back of the fabric).

2. Insert the wire tails into the tunnel formed by the eye of the darner, through to the back of the fabric. Thread tails can also be taken through at the same time.

3. Gently pull the darner all the way through, leaving the wire tails in the hole.

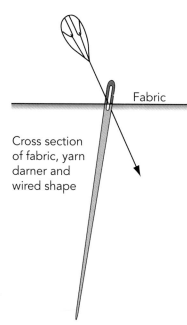

Fabric

Cross section of fabric, yarn darner and wired shape

4. Stitch the wire tails to the backing fabric with small stitches, preferably behind an embroidered area (make sure the securing stitches will be hidden behind embroidery or underneath a detached shape).

5. Use tweezers to bend the wired shape as required then trim the wire tails. I do not cut any wire tails until the subject is finished (just in case I need to unpick and re-do). Do not let any wire protrude into an unembroidered area as the tails may show when the piece is framed.

Working With Leather

Leather is available in a wide range of colours, thicknesses and finishes—fine kid, thicker leather, suede and snakeskin—and is used in stumpwork, goldwork and other areas of embroidery to provide a contrast in texture and colour.

To Cut a Leather Shape

Trace an outline of the required shape onto paper, a removable self-adhesive label or a Post-it note (make sure the sticky section is underneath the traced outline). Cut out the paper shape and apply to the leather to use as a template. Using small, sharp scissors cut the leather around the paper template with a long cutting motion (short cuts can cause an uneven edge or damage to the fine metallic coating of some leathers). If the leather is thick, it may be necessary to bevel the edges at the back. Do this with a sharp craft knife or scissors.

To Pad a Leather Shape

Leather is usually applied over a padding of one or more layers of felt. If more than one layer of felt is required to pad a shape, cut one piece of felt the actual size, and one or more successively smaller shapes. Applying the smallest shape first, attach each layer of felt with small stab stitches (coming out of the background fabric and stabbing into the felt), ending with the largest layer on top.

To Stitch Leather

Using a size 12 sharps needle and clear nylon thread (or fine silk thread in a matching colour), apply the leather with small stab stitches, bringing the needle out just under the edge of the leather, and stitching into the leather about 1–1.5 mm (1/16 in) from the edge (not too close to the edge or the leather may tear). The stitches should be worked fairly close together (1.5–2 mm apart) to avoid bulges between them, and need to be fairly firm to pull the sides of the leather down to hide the cut edge. Tweezers or the edge of a nail file (or a mellor), can be used to smooth and ease the edges of the leather into shape after it has been applied.

Finishing Techniques

The completed projects may be framed, mounted into a box or paperweight, or made into a brooch, bag or book cover. Stumpwork embroidery can also be mounted into the lids of gilt, porcelain and wooden bowls, and gilded brooch frames, all of which are readily available (made by Framecraft).

To Prepare Embroidery for Framing

I like to steam my work before removing it from the hoop or frame. I find that this process helps to tighten the background fabric and set or block the embroidery. There are several methods that can be used to generate steam—choose the method that suits you best. Make sure that you protect your hand with either a towel or rubber glove.

- Hold the hoop or frame over a steaming kettle, the wrong side of the embroidery facing the steam. Allow the steam to penetrate through to the front of the embroidery.

- If you have a reliable steam iron, hold the iron just above the back of your embroidery and allow the steam to penetrate through to the front. Place a clean tea towel over the back of the embroidery hoop, just in case there are any drips.

- Steam may also be produced by wrapping a damp towel around a dry iron and holding the iron just above the back of your embroidery, allowing the steam that is generated to penetrate through to the front of the embroidery.

- Allow your embroidery to dry in the frame overnight before removing.

To Lace Embroidery for Framing

REQUIREMENTS

- ✛ thick, white acid-free cardboard (or foam-core board)
- ✛ thin padding: cotton flannelette or Pellon
- ✛ acid-free double-sided adhesive sheet or tape
- ✛ glass-headed pins
- ✛ strong thread (e.g. Gutermann Polyester strong thread)
- ✛ strong needle

1. Cut the board to size and cover with a layer of padding, cut 2.5 cm (1 in) larger on each side than the board. Fold the turnings to the back of the board and attach with double-sided adhesive tape, trimming the corners.

2. Lay the embroidery face down on a padded surface (e.g. a folded fluffy towel) with a layer of white tissue paper in between to avoid damaging the raised elements.

3. Pin the calico/muslin backing to the edges of the board, checking that the embroidery is positioned correctly and that the tension is firm and even. Using strong thread, lace the two longer sides of the backing first, then the two shorter sides, trimming the corners for a neat finish.

4. Pin the main fabric to the edges of the board, making sure that the tension is even. Using strong thread, lace the two longer sides together first, then the two shorter sides, folding the corners in neatly.

5. Gently brush (or vacuum) the surface to remove any dust or stray threads, then arrange the detached elements (e.g.petals) as desired, using tweezers. To vacuum Cover the nozzle of the vacuum cleaner with organza. With the cleaner set on the minimum power, hold the nozzle just above the embroidery.

To Mount Embroidery into a Glass Paperweight

Framecraft paperweights are available in two sizes—small (54 mm) and large (72 mm). To enable these to be used for stumpwork embroidery, we have made wooden bases with a deep recess to accompany them.

REQUIREMENTS

- glass paperweight
- recessed wooden base of the appropriate size
- circle of acid-free cardboard (1.5 mm thickness)
- circle of thin padding (e.g. pellon) slightly smaller than cardboard circle
- strong thread (e.g. Gutermann Polyester strong thread)
- strong needle
- PVA adhesive
- clear silicone glue (e.g. Selleys Window and Glass Sealant)

1. Cut a circle of cardboard to fit inside the recess of the wooden base. Gather the embroidery firmly over the cardboard, enclosing the layer of thin padding, then lace with strong thread. Gather the main fabric and the muslin backing separately for a smoother finish.

2. Using PVA adhesive, glue the embroidery-covered cardboard into the recessed wooden base, pressing gently until it is secure.

3. Gently brush (or vacuum) the surface to remove any dust or stray threads and arrange the detached elements (e.g. petals) as desired, using tweezers.

4. Attach the glass paperweight to the wooden base with a thin layer of clear silicone glue (take care not to use too much). Leave under a weight until the sealant has cured.

5. Apply a circle of self-adhesive suede (or felt) to the base of the paperweight.

To Mount Embroidery into the Lid of a Gilt, Porcelain or Wooden Trinket Box

REQUIREMENTS

✛ porcelain, wooden or gilt trinket box or pincushion (Framecraft)
✛ circle of acid-free cardboard to fit inside the rim of the lid
✛ circle of thin padding (e.g. pellon) slightly smaller than cardboard circle
✛ strong thread (e.g. Gutermann Polyester strong thread)
✛ strong needle

1. Gather the embroidery firmly over the circle of cardboard, enclosing the layer of padding, then lace with strong thread. Gather the main fabric and the muslin backing separately for a smoother finish. Press the gathers flat with the point of an iron if desired.

2. Insert the embroidery into the gilt rim of the lid, then push the metal backing plate into place as instructed. Line the lid with the circle of suede provided.

To Mount Embroidery into a Small Gilt Brooch or Bowl

Small embroideries can be mounted into a Framecraft brass trinket box, pill box or brooch, with the following alterations to the assembly procedure.

REQUIREMENTS

✛ small gilt bowl or brooch
✛ circle of thin cardboard to fit inside the rim of the lid
✛ circle of thin padding (e.g. pellon) slightly smaller than the cardboard circle
✛ strong thread (e.g. Gutermann Polyester strong thread)
✛ strong needle

1. Carefully trim the calico/muslin backing of the embroidery to a circle slightly smaller than the cardboard template (or acetate circle) supplied.

2. Cut the main fabric into a circle with a small turning allowance. Gather the main fabric over the thin card (or acetate circle), enclosing a small circle of padding. Press the gathers flat with the point of an iron if desired.

3. Insert the embroidery into the empty frame then push the metal backing plate into place as instructed. Line the lid with the circle of suede provided

Equipment

The well-equipped workbox will contain:

✛ Good quality embroidery hoops—10 cm, 12 cm, 15 cm, 20 cm and 25 cm
(4 in, 5 in, 6 in, 8 in and 10 in). Bind the inner ring of wooden hoops with cotton tape to
prevent slipping. A small screwdriver is useful to tighten the embroidery hoops.
Plastic hoops with a lip on the inner ring are also suitable.

✛ Slate frames in various sizes for larger embroideries and goldwork

✛ Wooden tracing boards of various sizes—to place under hoops of fabric when tracing

✛ Needles (detailed information follows)

✛ Thimble

✛ Beeswax

✛ Fine glass-headed pins

✛ Embroidery scissors (small, with fine sharp points), goldwork scissors
(small and strong with sharp points) and paper scissors

✛ Small wire cutters or old scissors for cutting wire

✛ Mellor or old metal nail file (for easing threads or leather into place)

✛ Assortment of tweezers (from surgical suppliers)

✛ Eyebrow comb (for Turkey knots)

✛ Tracing paper (I use Glad Bake/baking parchment)

✛ Fine (0.5 mm) HB lead pencil (mechanical)

✛ Stylus or used ball-point pen (for tracing)

✛ Masking tape (for tracing and to hold threads and wire tails to the back of the fabric)

✛ Post-it notes or removable self-adhesive labels (for templates)

✛ Rulers—15 cm and 30 cm (6 in and 12 in).

Hint: Photocopy a small ruler and cut it out. This paper ruler is very useful for
goldwork and, when used on its side around a curve, for accurately positioning beads in a
border, for example, the Turkish Tulip Tile.

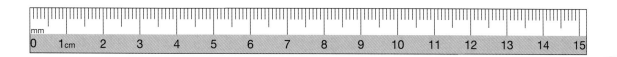

Needles

An assortment of needles is required. When selecting a needle, make sure that it is the appropriate type to suit the purpose. The thread should pass easily through the eye, and the needle should make a hole in the fabric large enough for the double thickness of the thread to pass through easily (without damaging the thread).

- **Crewel/embroidery sizes 3–10** Crewel needles are used with embroidery silks and cottons. They have a sharp point and long eye to take one or more strands of thread. Use a size 10 needle for one strand of thread, a size 9 for two strands (the more strands of thread, the larger the needle required).

- **Milliners/straw sizes 3–9** Milliners needles have a round eye and a long shaft that does not vary in diameter from its eye until it tapers at the point. They are ideal for working French and bullion knots, and for stitching with metallic embroidery threads (make sure the needle is thicker than the thread). A size 9 is used with one strand of fine metallic thread.

- **Tapestry sizes 24–28** Tapestry needles have an elongated eye and a blunt point which makes them ideal for working raised stem stitch and needle-weaving.

- **Sharps sizes 8–12** These are sharp needles with a round eye. Size 12 is ideal for stitching with fine machine threads, silk and nylon monofilament, and to apply leather and beads. Use the larger sizes when stitching with metallic thread—the thicker the thread the larger the needle required.

- **Beading sizes 10–13** These are very fine sharp needles with a long eye. Use to stitch beads with a very small hole (e.g. 1.5 mm gold pearls).

- **Chenille sizes 18–24** Chenille needles are thick and sharp and have an elongated eye. Use when stitching with thick thread (e.g. Soft Cotton), and for sinking some metallic threads through to the back.

- **Yarn darners sizes 14–18** Yarn darners are sharp and thick with a long eye. Use to insert detached wired shapes (e.g. petals and leaves), for sinking the tails of metal threads through to the back and for stitching very thick threads and chenille.

GLOSSARY OF
PRODUCT NAMES

This list gives equivalent names for products used
in this book which may not be available
under the same name in every country.

biro	ball-point pen
calico	muslin
clutch pencil	mechanical pencil
GLAD Bake	baking parchment
Pellon	thin polyester wadding
quilter's muslin	finely woven calico or cotton homespun
Vliesofix	paper-backed fusible web, Bondaweb

Stitch Glossary

This glossary contains most the stitches used in this book, in alphabetical order. For ease of explanation, some of the stitches have been illustrated with the needle entering and leaving the fabric in the same movement. When working in a hoop this is difficult (or should be if your fabric is tight enough), so the stitches have to be worked with a stabbing motion, in several stages.

Back Stitch

This is a useful stitch for outlining a shape. Bring the needle out at 1, insert at 2 (sharing the hole made by the preceding stitch) and out again at 3. Keep the stitches small and even.

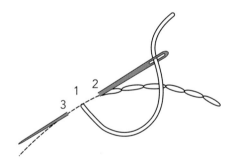

Back Stitch, Split

See Split Back Stitch

Buttonhole Stitch

These stitches can be worked close together or slightly apart. Working from left to right, bring the needle out on the line to be worked at 1 and insert at 2, holding the loop of thread with the left thumb. Bring the needle up on the line to be worked at 3 (directly below 2), over the thread loop and pull through to form a looped edge. If the stitch is shortened and worked close together over wire, it forms a secure edge for cut shapes, for example, detached petals.

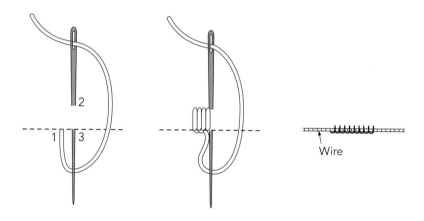

Buttonhole Stitch, Long & Short

In long and short buttonhole stitch, each alternate stitch is shorter. Bring the needle out at 1, insert at 2 and up again at 3 (like an open detached chain stitch). When embroidering a shape like a petal, angle the stitches towards the centre of the flower.

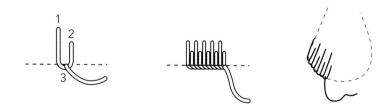

Chain Stitch

Bring the needle out at 1 and insert it again through the same hole, holding the loop
of thread with the left thumb. Bring the needle up a short distance away at 2, through
the loop, and pull the thread through. Insert the needle into the same hole at 2 (inside
the loop) and make a second loop, hold, and come up at 3. Repeat to work a row of chain
stitch, securing the final loop with a small straight stitch.

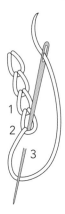

Chain Stitch, Detached
(Lazy Daisy Stitch)

Detached chain stitch or lazy daisy stitch is worked in the same way as chain stitch
except that each loop is secured individually with a small straight stitch. The securing
stitch can be made longer if desired. Several detached chain stitches can be worked
inside each other to pad a small shape.

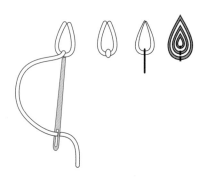

Couching

Couching is used to attach a thread, or bundle of threads, to a background fabric by means of small, vertical stitches worked at regular intervals. The laid thread is often thicker or more fragile (e.g. gold metallic) than the one used for stitching.

Couching stitches are also used for attaching wire to the base fabric before embroidering detached shapes.

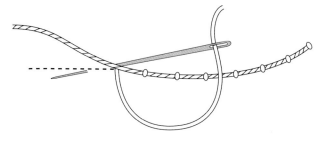

Couching, Lattice

Lattice couching is one of the endless variations of couched fillings. The design area is filled with a network of laid, parallel, evenly spaced threads. Where two threads cross, they are secured to the background with a small straight stitch.

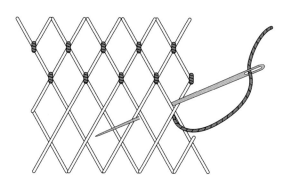

French Knot

Using a milliners/straw needle, bring the thread through at the desired place, wrap the thread once around the point of the needle and re-insert the needle. Tighten the thread and hold taut while pulling the needle through. To increase the size of the knot use more strands of thread, although more wraps can be made if desired.

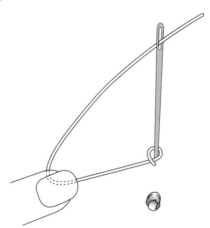

Long & Short Stitch

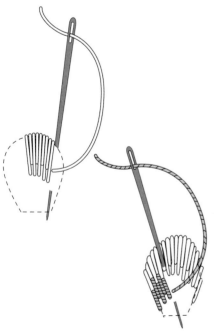

This stitch can be used to fill areas too large or irregular for satin stitch, or where shading is required. The first row, worked around the outline, consists of alternating long and short satin stitches (or long and short buttonhole stitch may be used). In the subsequent rows, the stitches are all of similar length, and fit into the spaces left by the preceding row. For a more realistic result when working petals, direct the stitches towards the centre of the flower. The surface will look smoother if the needle either pierces the stitches of the preceding row or enters at an angle between the stitches.

Long & Short Buttonhole Stitch

See Buttonhole stitch, long and short

Needle-Weaving

Needle-weaving is a form of embroidery where thread in a tapestry needle is woven in and out over two or more threads attached to the background fabric. Work needle-weaving over three threads for the Carnation petals.

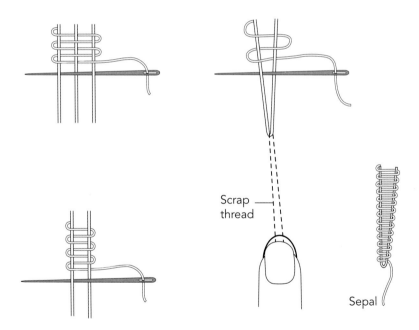

Scrap thread

Sepal

Overcast Stitch

This stitch is made up of tiny, vertical satin stitches, worked very close together over a laid thread or wire, resulting in a firm raised line. When worked over wire it gives a smooth, secure edge for cut shapes, for example, the detached Pear Flower petals. Place the wire along the line to be covered. Working from left to right with a stabbing motion, cover the wire with small straight stitches, pulling the thread firmly so that there are no loose stitches which may be cut when the shape is cut out.

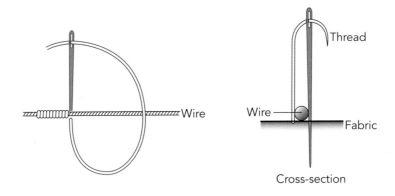

Pad Stitch

Pad stitch is used as a foundation under satin stitch when a smooth, slightly raised surface is required. Padding stitches can be either straight stitches or chain stitches, worked in the opposite direction to the satin stitches. Felt can replace pad stitch for a more raised effect.

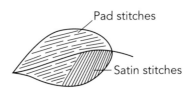

Satin Stitch

Satin stitch is used to fill shapes such as petals or leaves. It consists of horizontal or vertical straight stitches, worked close enough together so that no fabric shows through, yet not overlapping each other. Satin stitch can be worked over a padding of felt or pad stitches. Smooth edges are easier to achieve if the shape is first outlined with split stitch (or split back stitch).

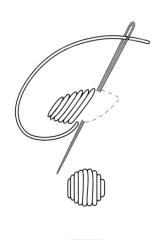

Split Stitch

Split stitch can be used either as an outline stitch or for smooth, solid fillings. Split stitch is worked in a similar way to stem stitch; however, the point of the needle splits the preceding stitch as it is brought out of the fabric. To start, make a straight stitch along the line to be worked. Bring the needle through to the front, splitting the straight stitch with the point of the needle. Insert the needle along the line then bring through to the front again to pierce the preceding stitch. Repeat to work a narrow line of stitching, resembling fine chain stitch.

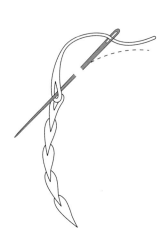

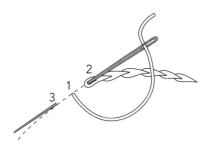

Split Back Stitch

An easier version of split stitch, especially when using one strand of thread. Commence with a backstitch. Bring the needle out at 1, insert at 2 (splitting the preceding stitch) and out again at 3. This results in a fine, smooth line, ideal for stitching intricate curves.

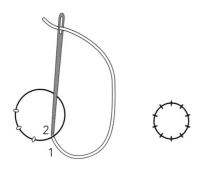

Stab Stitch

Stab stitch is used to apply leather or felt shapes to a background fabric. It consists of small straight stitches made from the background fabric over the edge of the applied shape, for example, a leather shape over felt padding. Bring the needle out at 1, and insert at 2, catching in the edge of the applied piece.

Straight Stitch

Individual straight stitches, of equal or varying length, can be stitched with a variety of threads to achieve interesting effects, for example, the Knapweed petals.

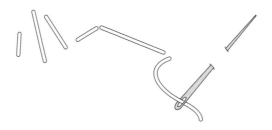

Bibliography & Further Reading

I gain an immense amount of pleasure from my books and can always justify the addition of another volume to the collection! I have referred to the following for information and inspiration.

Allan, James W. Islamic Ceramics. Ashmolean Museum, Oxford, 1991.

Atasoy, Nurhan & Raby, Julian. Iznik. Alexandria Press, London, 1989.

Baker, M. & Richardson, B. A Grand Design. V & A Publications, London, 1997.

Budden, Sue. Floral Ornament. BookKing International, Paris, 1995.

Canby, Sheila R. Islamic Art in Detail. The British Museum Press, London, 2005.

Christie, Archibald H. Pattern Design, Dover, New York, 1969.

Cole, Herbert. Heraldry: Decoration and Floral Forms. Crescent Books, New York, 1988.

Day, Lewis F. Ornament and Its Application. Batsford, London, 1904.

Day, Lewis F. Pattern Design. Batsford, London, 1903.

Durant, Stuart. Ornament. The Overlook Press, New York, 1986.

Hobhouse, Penelope. Plants in Garden History. Pavilion Books, London, 1992.

Jones, Owen. Decorative Ornament. Tess Press, New York, 2006.

Krody, Sumru B. Flowers of Silk and Gold. Merrell, Washington, DC, 2000.

Lang, Gordon. 1000 Tiles. A & C Black, London, 2004.

Meyer, Franz S. Meyer's Handbook of Ornament. Omega Books, London, 1987.

Midgley, W. and Lilley, A.E.V. Plant Form and Design. Chapman & Hall, London, 1916.

Paul, Tessa. Tiles for a Beautiful Home. Merehurst, London, 1989.

Pugin, Augustus W. Floriated Ornament. Richard Dennis, Somerset, 1994.

Rogers, J.M. The Arts of Islam. Art Gallery of NSW, Sydney, 2007.

Scott, Philippa. Turkish Delights. Thames & Hudson, London, 2001.

The Pepin Press. Persian Designs. Agile Rabbit, The Netherlands, 2002.

Trilling, James. The Language of Ornament. Thames & Hudson, London, 2001.

Ware, D. and Stafford, M. An Illustrated Dictionary of Ornament.
   Allen & Unwin, London, 1974.

EMBROIDERY

Christie, Grace. Samplers and Stitches. Batsford, London, 1920.

Enthoven, Jacqueline. The Stitches of Creative Embroidery. Schiffer, USA, 1987.

Thomas, Mary. Dictionary of Embroidery Stitches, Hodder & Stoughton, London, 1934.

STUMPWORK

Nicholas, Jane. Stumpwork Embroidery: A Collection of Fruits, Flowers, Insects.
   Sally Milner Publishing Pty Ltd, 1995.

Nicholas, Jane. Stumpwork Embroidery Designs and Projects.
   Sally Milner Publishing Pty Ltd, 1998.

Nicholas, Jane. Stumpwork Dragonflies. Sally Milner Publishing Pty Ltd, 2000.

Nicholas, Jane. Stumpwork, Goldwork and Surface Embroidery: Beetle Collection.
   Sally Milner Publishing Pty Ltd, 2004.

Nicholas, Jane. The Complete Book of Stumpwork Embroidery.
   Sally Milner Publishing Pty Ltd, 2005.

Nicholas, Jane. Stumpwork Medieval Flora. Sally Milner Publishing Pty Ltd, 2009.

Picture Credits

END PAPERS PANEL OF FRITWARE TILES WITH AN ARCH MOTIF; TURKEY (PROBABLY IZNIK),
   1570–74. *V & A Diary 2007.* V & A Enterprises Ltd, London, 2007 (image opp. May 14
   Week 20). Victoria & Albert Museum, London.

PAGE 9 BORDER OF CERAMIC TILES; PERSIA, SIXTEENTH CENTURY. Image taken from
   Persian Designs. Agile Rabbit, The Netherlands, 2002 (p. 75). Published by The
   Pepin Press.

PAGE 10 GLAZED EARTHENWARE TILE IN THE FORM OF A TWELVE-POINTED STAR; IRAN, C. 1444. *V & A Diary 2007*. V & A Enterprises Ltd, London, 2007 (image opp. Oct 22 Week 43). Victoria & Albert Museum, London

PAGE 67 PANEL OF FRITWARE TILES DEPICTING A ROW OF NICHES CONTAINING VASES OF FLOWERS; Turkish (probably Iznik), seventeenth century. *V&A Images*, Victoria and Albert Museum, London

PAGE 128 TEXTILE WITH POMEGRANATE PALMETTE MOTIF; Persian, sixteenth century. Image taken from *Persian Designs*. Agile Rabbit, The Netherlands, 2002 (p.48). Published by The Pepin Press.

PAGE 178 PEN BOX AND UTENSILS; INDIAN (MUGHAL), EIGHTEENTH CENTURY. Baker, M. & Richardson, B. A Grand Design. *V & A Publications*, London, 1997 (p.247). Victoria & Albert Museum, London

PAGE 192 OTTOMAN SQUARE PANEL. Image taken from *Persian Designs*, Agile Rabbit, The Netherlands, 2002 (p.112). Published by The Pepin Press.

PAGE 198 PANEL DECORATED WITH ARABESQUE PATTERN, PERSIAN. Image taken from *Persian Designs*, Agile Rabbit, The Netherlands, 2002 (p.33). Published by The Pepin Press.

PAGE 208 BORDER OF TURKISH TILES. Image taken from *Persian Designs*, Agile Rabbit, The Netherlands, 2002 (p. 96). Published by The Pepin Press.

PAGE 208 BORDER OF TURKISH TILES. Image taken from *Persian Designs*, Agile Rabbit, The Netherlands, 2002 (p. 97). Published by The Pepin Press.

PAGE 234 PAGE OF ORNAMENTED ARCHITRAVES AND UNDER-SURFACES OF WINDOWS IN THE INTERIOR OF THE MOSQUE OF TOOLOON, CAIRO. Jones, Owen. *Decorative Ornament*. Tess Press, New York, 2006 (Plate XXXI p.136). Image courtesy, University of Wisconsin Digital Collections.

PAGE 236 EXAMPLES OF ARABIAN ORNAMENT FROM SANCTA SOPHIA. Jones, Owen. Decorative Ornament. Tess Press, New York, 2006 (p.132). Image courtesy, University of Wisconsin Digital Collections.

PAGE 221 AL-MAHDIYAR MAP (MS. Arab. c. 90, fol. 34a Ch. 2.13 © Bodleian Library, University of Oxford). Emilie Savage-Smith and Yossef Rapoport(eds.), *The Book of Curiosities: A Critical Edition*. World-Wide-Web publication. (www.bodley.ox.ac.ukbookofcuriosities) (March 2007)

Embroidery Supplies
& Kit Information

The threads, beads and needlework products referred to in this book are available from Jane Nicholas Embroidery and specialist needlework shops.

A mail order service is offered by Jane Nicholas Embroidery. Visit the website and view the entire range of stumpwork kits, books and embroidery supplies including wires, fabrics, leather, beads, hoops, needles and scissors.

Thread ranges include Au Ver à Soie, Cifonda, chenille, DMC, Kreinik, Madeira and YLI, and goldwork supplies. Framecraft brooches, boxes and paper-weights are stocked for finishing. A mail order catalogue is available on request.

Jane Nicholas Embroidery

PO Box 300

Bowral NSW 2576

AUSTRALIA

T/F: +61 2 4861 1175

email: jane@janenicholas.com

www.janenicholas.com

ENDPAPERS *Panel of fritware tiles depicting a row of niches containing vases of flowers; Turkey (probably Iznik), seventeenth century.*